How Americans Must Deal Wtih A New Wave of Crime

by

Steven C Peete

AuthorHouse™
1663 Liberty Drive, Suite 200
Bloomington, IN 47403
www.authorhouse.com
Phone: 1-800-839-8640

First published by AuthorHouse 2/13/2009

ISBN: 978-1-4389-2961-3 (sc)

Printed in the United States of America
Bloomington, Indiana

This book is printed on acid-free paper.

authorнouse®

Table of Contents

Prefect

It seems like ever day we open our morning newspaper or turn owr tv sets we see, or read about crime. Crime, crime nothing but crime. The crimnal Element is taking over. Crime is up from car jacking to domestic vilence, spouce abuse, child abuse, white collar crime, ect. More and more people are reporting insedence of vilent crime. Crime unforuntaly has become part of owr dailey lives which cause millions od people miser, and heat ache. Everone is effected in this diesese called crime. And everone is suspected. This book will empasize certain element of crime, and some sulutions to this vase problem. The crimes seen in the past. And the sulutions to this problem. needs more careful study! The sulution of the crime problems of so to 100 years ago, wont work today. Politicion and state legistratures must take a hard look at crime. And place it high on there protity list. We are living in a new age, and a new time. And the crimes of today are called new wave.

Seincerly
Steven Peete
President

Introuduction

The threat of violent crime has reached epidemic portions. Violent crime is exacting a fearful toll in the communities of owr nation. Millions of people are being held hostage by their fear of crime, and violence. Though violent crime can strike anyone. Crime uslly strike people who live in the innercity. Crime has become the most importent issue confrunting. American cities and those who must live, or work within them. Yet most of our efforts to combat crime are futile, and at worst actually have the opposite effect of contributing to its increase. Some people sompare the vilence in Amerca, to the war in bosnia. Or the 1994 gencide in Cuanda. Yours truly has been a victem of vilent crime. And being a victem of vilent crime is something you will never forget. The best minds in the world try to solve the vrime problem over the past hundreds of years, nearly every solution they have come up with have falled. The sencless vilence from geneation to generation never ends. In ever aspect of owr lives criminal are rebaling agianst owr system. We as people must find new ways to deter, or control crime. So owr genertion of the future don't have to endor war. The same crime ways we are experienceing now. Theres more vilence today then ever before. And most vilence accurs because of people mistrust for one another. This is the only country were a person live can be taken by knokin on the wrong door. We as a group of human beings must know to trust one another, after all we are a homagery group, with the only diffrence is color, and size and opinion of how society should be ran. Community across the contry are tired of gangs and drugs. And they won't action taken to stop this virus. Law abiding citizens want to be able to walk the street in peace. Without worring about being born today will not reach there live expectise. Because of the high crime rate in most citys. The hurt and miser crime cause million of Amercan is unthinkable we are livin within a time bomb. Were everyone is ready to explode. In a country which is in turmoil. Crimnanal are becomeing a burden in ever aspected of live. People patients are short, and they want concred. The united states is still the strongest country in the world. And the problem of crime should have been solved years ago. If our country is to survey well into the next centry, we must learn to be better people as a hole, which includeds all the crimanl as well. We need ever person to be prouductive members of society so our society can continue to survive. No one person can save the world, but he, or she can make it a better place by saying no to crime, no to drug and violence. Now let look at crime as hole, from begining to end. We will look at some sultion to the crime problem when it started who are some of the people whos to blame, and can the problem ever be solved.

When did the crime Problem Start in Amerca

When you look at the crime problem in Amerca today you must look at the origintion of crime. Crime had been a problem in Amerca since the pilgram first landed at Plymouth rock back in the early 16 hundrends. Back then, criminal were hanged for crim such as robbery, rape, murder, asulted, ect. Know we as a people are more civilized and our courts desice how to punish offenders. Crime did not grow in our country untill the population expaned. The population grow after the industrly revelotion around 1700. The infux of criminal came from country were they were no work. Most of the criminal ended up in large cityslum looking for jobs. When there was no jobs, most of them turn to crime. New laws had to be enacted. Threw out the coloneys because of the canging groups of people. Although reform movements had managed to reduce criminal behavior, and some of the more blatant forms crime was still a problem. In the 1800's new forms of crime, and vice emerged as the older cities continued to grow and new ones were developed. By the 1840's criminal gangs criminal districts, and vice areas had become established in the older urban centers. After the Civil War, New York entered the age house of prostitution dance hall concert sploons, and gambling casinos operated openly throught the city. This open operation was linked to regular payment to corrupt police and political overloards. The political machines thrived on the extension of the police protection to virtually every form of vice and crime. In short, the road of crime lie deep in our past. Recognized as a social problem as early as the 1630's crime has assumed a varitey of forms street crimes, criminal districts, and vice areas, marked the older urban preps. In addition to its long experience with crime American society has also known much violence. Although you might think that violence is a part of crime, a second look suggests other wise. Much violence is never reacted to as if it were a criminal in fact it may be socially permitted either way, the united states has witnessed a great amount of violence. Violence can be seen as an act which involves killing, or injuring people, or significantly damaging property, it might seem unusual to consider siolence separetly from crime how ever in this country violence has been used afainst religious dissenters, Indians in dentuired servents and slaves. The Unites states was born in the violence of revolution at the same time, all citizens were given a consitutional right to bear arms Dueling lynching, blood feuds, and riots have all been part of American life. In fact, some of the violence that has characterized American society has occurred in the reaction to crime, whether officially in law enforcement, or unofficially in vigilante movements Those are two major forms of American violence, intergroup violence which sets one group against another, and interpersonal violence which involves individuals. Both forms appear to lack cohesion the targets issues people, and places involved, and affected differ greatly. Both appear to be associated with a remarkable mass amnesia most of our violent past has been completely forgotten or left for historions to uncover at a later time.

Aside from the violence brought about by groups taking the law into their own hands. The unites states has experienced many types of violent confrontation between diverse groups Political violence, econmic violence, racial, and ethnic violence, religious violence and radical violence, and police violence are all part of our heritage Yet it is not worthy that a great deal of American violence has been initiated on a canservative biosis, that is by established groups who felt themselves threated by outsideers such as cptholics radical workers, blacks, asians, and other ethnic racial or monerity. As you can see, crime effects all people from all backgrounds. And sence the country was started, theres always been people pointing fingers at each other. Crime has been a problem all threw owr history. People with different veiws, and there ways of doing things. Has upset the balance off crime over the past two hundred years or so. Most crime came from mistrust from one group over another, blacks against white, Liberols virse conservetive, republican over demacrates. All this must cange is we are to go forward

into the next mulleinem without this same kaous of crime we are going
threw today.

What motivates people to commted crime

As we have seen, the begin of crime in Amercan is based upon a varity of reasons different believe, live style, diffrent ethnic groups, diffrent religious beleive ect. The breif reveiw I've giving you, about the begin of crime, and vilence is only part of the many reason why crime has been a problem though out our history. If you need a in depth view of the beginning of the crime in Amerca check your library for more books on the subject of crime in vilence. There should be plenty of book on the subject with diffrent authers opinions. These authers will give you a braoder prospective of the problem. A second look at crime would be what motivates people to commted crime. After all there would not be a crime problem in Amerca if there was not people to do the crimes on any given day. There are over a million people, or more in our country which commited some sort of crime, be it demestic cilence, bank robbery, or stealing a car ect. What ever the crime may be. Crime are commited daily. What motivates people to commied crime is a hole nother matter. No one kews want goes threw a persons mind and why they do the things they do. What motivates a person to brake the law is any bodys guess. Most crimeogest believe, people motivation to crime is caused be a number of reason. Heres a list of the most common reason people commited crime:

1)<u>Money</u>= Robbery, Forgery and counterfeiting, Embezzlement, ect

2)<u>Power</u>= Politics, "example watergate brakein"

3)<u>Love</u>= Jealeosy of another to be rejected from another.

4)<u>Sex</u>= Rape, sexafender, child meslester horexcauiolity prostution ect.

5)Jealeosey= of what other people have, money success, looks ect.

6)Drugs= Drug sddicts, drifters ect.

Money seems to be the number one reason why crimes are commited in the united states. After interveiw hundreds of police office and detectives (personl) robbery, bank robbery, forgery, and conterfeideing, creditcards, embezzlement ect, is on the rise all over the country. The people who cummit these crime have no refarded for the police, or the people who they use these crimes against. Here is a breif reveiw of robbery (personal) bank, forgery and counterfeiting, and embezzlement and the highest of these crimes, on our society.

Bank Robbery= There are 2 thousand bank robberys every day, threwout the united state. The average take of each robbery is around 2,500 dollors. Bank robbery has been a problem in the united state for years. Each state has there own way of handling robbery but in most state bank robbery is a felony. But that does not seem to deter the common criminal. The average bank robbery is black between the ages of 25 to 30. These robbers are hard to detect, because most police don't know where or when they are going to strike. Acording to the F.B.I bank robber cost tax payer million of dollors is a dispprity crime, for disparty people. Yes money is importent, we all need money to pay our bill but, to brake the law for some money sound ludicrous. But we all don't think the same, and do the same thinks. In my opionion, bank robbery should put away there childish ways and act like adult, and get a real job.

Robbery- After bank robbery, second highest crime is robbery against a person. Such as purse snaching, wallet stolen pick pockets, creditcards ect. The crime robbery has occurred when there has been completed theft with the use of force, or threat of use of force. There force, if there has been a taking (capture) and carrying away asportation of property with intent to deprive the owner permently of possession, there has been a theift. These type of theft are also hard to detect. Most people who commit these crime are in the lower economic bracket. In most state these crime carry find, or imprisment or both.

Strong armed robbery, such as mugging and joking (or simple robbery) is distinguished in all states statutes from the aggravated form of robbery, commonly called armed robbery. Armed robbery carries penalities more severe than those for a simple robbery. Some of the statutory distinctions used by various states in distinguishing between armed robbery and

> (1) simple robbery are that the perpertrator was armed with a dangerous or deadly weapons.

> (2) that the perpetrator intended to kill or wound if the victam resisted.

Most state take armed robbery very serious. Many people have lost there lives in stickup by scurrilous crimnal. Armed robbery is growing in ever major city. And the police department in those citys . May have to retrain there police office to deal with the new bread of stickup men, and women who are out there know.

Forgery- Documents and writing are importent in the functioning of a modern society. The crimes of forgery and uttering are offenses, created primarily to safe guard confidence in the genuineress of documents and writing forgery is committed when a person with an intent to defraud flalsely makes, or alters a writing, or document. Forgery may be committed by, creeating a wholly new false writing, or document altering an existing writing or document raising the amount of a check would be an example endorsing a check, or other instrument with another persons name. Check forging rings operate in all large cities in the united state in many instance these rings obtain checks from business and industrial firms as a result of burglaries by means of check writing machines and type writers, the stolen checks are then forged to appear as pay roll checks. The checks are often forged using names found on stolen identification cards, and papers. Such identification can be obtained by purse snathing and pick pocketing. Forgery is a crime which has been around for hundreds of years. And will be around hundreds of years from know. This is another crime in which police have to be retraining in. Do to the computer age, crooks are learning the trade of forgery by using highteck equipment such as lazer printers and the like, be careful make sure you are not a victem of this crime of forgery. To protect yourself itgninst other crime follow these guidelines.

(1) Make sure you dont leave important document out for people easy espaser

(2) Make sure you destroy carbons leaet out with you signer on them.

(3) Make sure you keep important document with you signer locked up.

(4) Dont trust no one with your important paper insurance, checkbook, ect creditcard pin number

p330 Crimnal Law Thomas, J Gardner

If you following my guide lines. You will lessing your chances of being a victem of forgery you will be glad you did.

Counterfeiting- of currency and coins is a serious federal offence which keep the secret service bussy these days. The history of conterfeiting in the united states can be summerized as follow Untill and during the civil war, conterfeiting was a serious problem as thousands, of diffrent legal bills were printed by more than 2,000 state banks. It is estimated that as much as on third of the currency used during the Civil War was counterfeit. Conterfeiting was easy during that period Establishment of a single national currency in 1863 and oception of the U.S. secret service immediately made conterfeiting difficult. Counterfeiting the new currency required highly skilled persons with highly sophisticated equipment. The diligent efforts of the secret service made the pooling of the neccessary material and equipment plus the necessary highly trained skills difficult. Conterfeiting and alterations of currency were kept at a minimum over the years. Today conterfeiting has increased as a crime because new printing, and copying equipment and methods have made it possible for less sophisticated individuals to become conterfeiters, much of the conterfeiters of Amercan money is done out side the united state, and is ether passed off to others abroad, or smuggled into the united state.

Embasslement- Is another form of theft, and lerceny. In this offence, the thief has legal possession of a property or negotiable intruments of another. But uses, converts, or retains the property fraudulently, usually to his or her own use or to the use of someone other than the owner. Some states list the various types of persons who might have lawful possession of property belonged to the city a school, a corporation, or an individual would suffice. Since the consent of the owner would constitute a total defense in a theft or larceny charge, the owner must testify that the taking was with out his, or her consent. A showing that the owner did not consent to the conduct of the defendant is also neccessary in criminal damage to property, in trepass, and in avson of ether real or personal property. The statutes of many states provide that the crime of embezzlement can also be committed by state, or local officials who have public funds in their possession It is also common to divide embezzlement into ground embezzlement a (felony) and petit embezzlement a misdemeanor as with larceny and theft, a series of small fraudulent conversions over a period of time that are part of a single scheme may be charged as one large embezzlement. There are crimes which potain to money such as creditcards, goverment contracts medicar extortion, shoplifting and computer crimes, ect all these are on the rise. But it will be up to state, and city goverments to put these crime to an end. Before the problem get tottal out of control.

Crimes for power- All threw our history there have been crimes for power. Most of these crime occur in the political ring. One of the most famaus cases is the watergate brake in the early 1970's. In political crimes the symbolic meaning of the criminal act is more important than the act it self. Former president Richard Nixon's characterization of the watergate brake in as a third-rate burglary was true except for a most important fact that it was committed on behalf of the committee to reelect the president. Since meaning is more important than act in the definition of political crime, assessing its scope and social importance can be most difficult and at times arbitary. The other side of this political crimes involves goverment breaking its own laws This can be done in two ways (1) The power of an agency or office can be done used against citizens, or against the public interest, and (2) the

8

holder of an office can use it for personal gain. Again, the range of acts is as wide as crime in general Violence theft, deceit, violation of civil rights, and even sexual abuse may be involved although governmental law breaking has occured for centuries, only in the past decades has it become a focus for subtained criminological attention. The public exposure of watergate, and subsequent revelations of lawlessness by government agencies have meant that everyone is aware of this form of political crime Governmental over prosecution of dissent discussed in trhe preceding section could be interpreted as abuse of office. The second type of abuse of office involves situation in which the holder of an office use it for personal gain. Commonly called "corruption", this type of abuse has been the subject of comment ever since people held positions of power. Curiously, it has long been studied by political scientists but only recently by criminologest. Perhaps this is because of a split among criminologist about how crime of corruption should be perceived while some would give corruption an important place in the study of political crime, others would prefer to see it as a species of property offence rather then as political crimes committed with a political objective transcending individual aggrandizement, but the point is that the theifts, and other crimes involved in corruption are possible only because of the political office that is held. On the state and local levels corruption appears to be even more common than on the federal level. It is here that political machines have thrived. Political corruption will always be with us. The only way to change political corruption is to change the political envirment.

Love- Crimes for love has been around sence there has been man and woman. These crimes usually involved boy friend, and girl friend or husband and wife. Spouces abuse is problem all over the country. Most abuser say its because of love. But satistics say otherwise. There are over 1 million women each year who are beating by there husband and boy friend. Crimes from rejected spouce is a problem in todays world, if you love your spouce you will not beat on them, or harse them. When the relationship is over learn to go your own way.

Sex Crimes- There are many sex crime in the law books. In all 50 state. Crimes such as rape, childmolstiory homosexuality, and prostitution,

9

are the most populare one. The united states has attempted to control various aspect of sexual behavior. The degree of consent, the nature of the object or person the nature of the sexual act, and the setting in which the act occurs for the most part, laws concerning consent have to do with forcible rape. However, there are also laws against consensual relations between minors against intercourse between adult males and minor females, and against sexual coercion of minors by adults. Concerning persons, about half of our states have laws against extramarital intercourse. All forbid incest sexual relationship under criminal law. The nature of sexual acts prohibited under the criminal law is also very inclusive. The majority of states have laws against sodomy oral-genital and anal genital contacts, even between husband, and wife are illegal in most states, and today they still carry severe penalities in many states some states laws regard any position for intercourse other than the conventianal one of man laying on the woman as a crime against nature more over, as recently as 1996, the Supreme Court up held the right of states to make laws that regulate the private sexual behavior of consenting adults. Finally the law has attempted to regulate the setting in which the sexual act occurs. Prostitution the granting of sexual access on a relatively indiscriminate basis for payment is illegal in every state except Nevada, where counties can decide to allow brothels if they so choose other criminal laws are more specifically focused on those who would maintain a house of prostitution, on pimps who would exploit prostitution for their own personal gain, and on procurers who seek to lure other into prostitution.

(more about prostitution later in book)

Jealousy- Jealousy is a crime which occurs between the haves and have nots in a society which offers everything for there people. Destrobution of wealth is still a problem. There is still large portion of poverty threwout the united states. (mostly in citys) People are jealous because you may have a better job. A successful business a new car, successful doctor, or lawyer ect. As the saying goes keep up with the jones is true.

Drugs- The use of drugs whether to achive relaxation, and pleasure or to treat illness has long been part of human condition. Yet it is

10

only within the past century, or so that drug addiction and abuse have been regarded as a major social problems although governments have attempted to criminalize various aspects of the use of drugs, there are substantial numbers in the population who continue their drug-consuming habits in violation of the criminal law. The specifics of drug use and abuse are complex in part because of the tremendous scientific advances over the past several decades. (more about drug later in book) Finall there are other reason why people committed crimes such as bordem, tension in home infirment, jobs, or just for the thrill of it. What ever the reason crime has to be altered. So we as people can go forward without crime and violence.

Who Are the Criminals

Criminal today come from diversty backround they are black, white, young, and old profesinal and non profesinal. They are located in all 50 state. Criminal are angry, disturbed people who are looking for attention. Thirty to forty years ago it wasnt like that. Criminals no longer just grab hand bags. They shoot people. They rob the state, then go back and shoot the clerk. Public figures are involved in all kinds of corruption. People dont seem to care for one another anymore. Criminals are more heartless and vicious. In this section I will try to pinpont (1)How people become criminals (2)who are the criminals (3)The cost of criminal to our society.

(1)How people become criminals- To look at how people become criminals you must look at there backrounds, and how they were raised studying individual offenders began in the 1850's when officials started to examine biographies of prisoners in the attempt to understand why they had turned to crime. It flourished in the latter 1800's when criminologest turned to scientific positiuism, which sought to use the methodolgy of the emerging natural sciences to understand, to predict, and to attempt to control criminals over the years, many thearies have been advanced. As we shall see, some have been disproved, others have been discarded, and still others have given rise to more complex formulations criminological positivists argue that the cause of crime are to be found in the personal characteristic of offenders in this argument, there are two interolated assumptions (1)that offenders are different from non offenders (2)and that offenders are led into or imes by forces over which they have less than complete control. Many developmental specialists agree that violence interrupt the usual growth of empothetic feelings that is neccessary for moral reasoning ordinarily, such thinking begins at the age of 4 or 5. And comes from attachments to parents, and others who teach children limits and trust, and who demonstrate love, and understanding. Children learn to care for others and to distinguish right from wrong at this stage by internalizing the care they receive themselves, and applying it in relationships with others. If you cut short that process with an environment of emotional change, the valve of live, and moral conduct are gone. Many killer are victims of awful child abuse. In a study published by the American Academy of child and Adolescent Phychiatry in 1988 found that 12 of 14 juveniles on death row in four states had long histories of severe beating, and sexual abuse, mostly by drug addicted parents. These attacks possibly caused changes in their begin chemistry, and prompted violent behavior as the children grew the study found that maltreatment, in childrens inclination to act impulsively, to be extremely wary of the world, and to misperceive threats and often caused children to lose the ability to feel empathy for others abuse also diminished both their judgement, and their verbal competence making children less able to express what they feel or what happens to them if a person is chronically stressed, the biological changes that occur make them less able to control their behavior, and more likely to lash out. Other research suggests that witnessing violence can inspire long term rage. Sometimes, when young children witness unchecked ciolence against someone they know, they later fantasize about intervening to save someone they care about furious at their inability to stop the violence. They seem glazed, and indifferent when, in fact, they are imprisoned in "terror". Murderous violence rarly arises from a single impulsive moment. Rather, it is often the culmination of years of escalating aggressive acts. The American Phycological Association, and the Justice Department released separate studies that show several developmental path ways leading boys to violence as the cruelty progresses children develop "habits of thought" that rule out calmer ways to settle disputes. Most commonlgy it starts with stubborn behavior, and defiance and 12 to annoying, or bullying other or between ages 12 and 14, it becomes into minor antisocial behavior like liying and cheating, and fighting with other boys. Then it grows into full blown, almost relentless violence. As the individual grow older into there late teens. There violence becomes rage, and rage becomes hate, hate turns into murder. These are the reasons children are dying in Americas mean streets at the hands of other children sneakers and lambskin coats, scuffles over pocket change, and of course drug turf in some cases, kids are slain just for hell of it. Heartless killer, and habitual criminal have always existed but the number of killings by younger, and younger kids has been scandalously little research into the phenomenon, so experts can offer only a guess at why the numbers of such crimes has grown so much since the mid 1980's. The growth of single parent family do to devorce. The escalation of weapons on the streets, and the despair caused by massive loss of urban manufacturing jobs. The result in ecology of terror that has turned many poor neighhoods into war zoon. The children of these places show many of the symptoms of kids in war torn lends including post traumatic stress emotional numbness, depression anxiety, and rage. A number of studies in the recent years shows that few of the youths who kill are psychotic in growing up, many are animated by a chillingly rational response to enviroment that is saturated with violence and stress where it is safe to trust no one, and where there is no sence of the future. How people become criminals is a version of response. But in my opinion home infirment is very important with good up bringing, and parental guidence during the first years of live. The criminal element in most people would not be there. If parents could motivate there children to go the right way such as school, church, work ect. Most but not if all criminals would not be in state prison, or in up on death row. Young minds need adults to motivate them, and show them the right way to go. Also community leaders must help motivating. People in their community to work together to keep young children away from gangs, and to grow up to be productive members of society. Instead of another statistics. The second important element of crime is who are the criminals. Criminals are people from all walks of live. They turn to crime for many reasons. In this section I'll place emphasis on these elements such as the following;

(1) Age of most criminals - juveniles crime problem

(2) Race of criminals black, white ect.

(3) Gender-male, female - criminal

(4) Hate Groups - Maliten groups, skin head, Klux Klux Klan

(5)Homeless Americans - Mental illness, criminal

(6)The cost of criminals: Jails, business orginization, courts

Age of most criminals - Criminal ages can range from 5 to 100. most criminal start there criminal activities at a very young age. In the united state, most of our criminals are young teenagers between the age of 15-17 satistic very from state to state about age. But according to police records. Juveniles seem to cause police the most problems. Until recently, the united state has been faced with continued increases in the size of young people between the age of 15-17 year-old population in fact between 1960- and 1970 the number of people in this age group, which is highly prone to crime, grew over 42 percent to more than 15 million although the number appears to have leveled off during the 1070's the sheer size of the youngful population has been a factor in the increases in recorded crime after 1960. Table 1, p19.

Criminal rate per thousand	1970	1985	Percentage
Murder and nonegligent manslaughter	930	1,057	+13.7
Forcable rape	2,355	2,691	+14.3
Robbery	18,981	25,480	+34.2
Aggravated assault-	14,393	23,541	+63.6
Burglery-	112,837	148,498	+31.8
Larceny-theft-	222,968	293,783	+31.8
Motor vehichle -	59,858	45,648	+23.7
Violent crimes-	36,659	52,769	43.9
Property crimes-	395,656	487,933	23.5
Crime index total-	432,315	540,702	25.1

Juveniles today are handled differently and separately from adults in almost every phase of the criminal justice system. Extensive use of differential treatment, and the exercise of discretion by individual officials at various stages of the criminal process cloud the juvenile crime picture. Some major adjustment have taken place in the juvenile system in the past few years, and more will probably be initiated in the future.

Detention for Juveniles - In all states, the major type of facility for juvenilies is the detention home where juvenile victim of crimes are kept in the same facilities as juvenile offenders with the same treatment afforded both. Many states have statutory provisions for the detention of juveniles in jails as long as they are segregated from adult offenders some states have stautes, or policies prohibiting the detention of juveniles in jails, but practical problems require the frequent violation such statutes. Facilities designated exclusively for juvenile detention are usually not the best examples of how an ideal juvenile correctional facility should be designed, and operated. Most of these structures were originally build for some other person, and converted to that present use with as little expenditure as possible. The average capacity of juvenile detention facilities is about sixty-one, but most are overcrowded before they reach that number. In the adult institutions the emphasis is on custody, and the same preoccupation with security shapes the programs, and the general environment in the juvenile detentions facilities most of them are located in urban areas, and are virtually sealed off from the community by their physical structure and other security measures. The youths are placed in a dormity-style housing, or single cells in some cases, of ten with the fixed furniture, and dreary interiors that are typical of adult institutions. Most juvenile detention centers lack services and programs that might improve the residents change of staying away from crime. Those juveniles are denied most of the good from adult programs. According to the 1977 census of public juvenile facilities, approximately 45,900 individual juveniles were housed. Within state, and local government facilities on December 31 1988, while the number of facilities at the end of 1988 four out of ten of which could be classified as open as opposed to institutionalized. And must significantly, almost two thirds of all long-term or past placement facilities were of the open type. The whole issue of whether it is productive to place juveniles in institutions is being hotly debated in correctional groups. One state has closed all of its juvenile institutions and others are phasing them out as soon as is practical verious supreme court decisions in the 1960 and 1970 have influenced the programs of the state traning schools to some extent, but many continue to operate with business-as usual Institutions are the most expensive and least successful method of handling juvenile offenders. But until the services needed to provide supervision and treatment in the community are forthcoming judges often have no other choice but to commit offenders. The junior prisons are not all bad, but the custody philosophy is the preupiling model, and it creates the same problem at this level as the adult level. The juvenile crime problem is one of the great concern, with the number of juveniles involved in serious crime increasing each year. The number of juvenile cases reaching the courts is also increasing in 1970's and 1980's the number of cases that reached the courts increased by 7 percent while informally handled cases increased only 3 percent in 1985 almost 1,000,000 juvenile offender cases were refered to juvenile court. It is recognized that community alternatives give the offender a better chance that the court proccesses, and the decline in their use compared with the use of the courts in a serious matter. Because the nature of a juveniles initial contact with the law is know to affect the like I herd of recidiuism, the moment in the juvenile justice system has been toward non judicial alternatives. In take screening and other motheds for diverting all but a few of the juveniles from official sanctioning in the judicial system is an important trend. This kind of service is most commenly described as informal adjustment, and informal probation because of the informal nature of such procedures, little is know as to their effectiveness. This is not neccessarily a handicap, however as the basic reason for closing most of these cases after a period of informal handling is that no further problems have arisen with the juvenile.

Reform movement to Get tough on Juveniles-

some state are using new and inproved method to curtain the raise of juvenile crime. Clearly, there is the perception and the reality among people, also among juvenile offenders that the juveniles codes is very lenient, and weak for years juveniles have used there age to commited adult crime such as, murder rape and assult ect Must state legislater, owe considering droping the age of conseed from 18 to 17 the age at which defendents would be tried as adults It also would lower from 12 to 10 the age at which children could be considered delinguents, and locked in a state-run fecility. Other key provisions (1)are Permit the filing of adult murder charges against children as young as 10 years old current laws allows for adult those 12 and older (in some state) Deny jury trial for juveniles who are not waived to adult court. (4)automatically waive delinquents to adault court if they were previously waived from juvenile court. (5)Permit juvenile offenders to be sentenced to 30 days in a juvenile detention center, or the juvenile wing of a county jail the country boards would first have to approve this sentencing opinion (in those county) Impose stiffer penalties for youngsters who commit drug-related crimes or crimes with guns, children caught illegally carrying a handgun could be jailed overnight. (6)widen access to juveniles court records such as judges would be required to disclose to anyone who requests them all court records except those that have sensitive personalty Information on juveniles. The current juvenile codes (in most state) which was drafted in the late 60's eaily senty. provides courts with a variety of options for trying to rehabilitate juvenile offenders. Those provisions will remain on the books under the legislation, But the code has proved inadepuate to adress the recent increase in the number of serious crimes commited by youg people. New laws will finally bring our juvenile laws into the present and well into the next century, we are no longer dealing with children who steal from coner store. we're dealing with kids who kill, and new bills finally addresses that problem. But critics contend the get tough legislation is to harsh. Serious juvenile offenders account for 10 to 15% of the children in the justice system. Yet changes in bill (in most state) all children accused of a crime under new legislation such as a 16 year old could stealing a car could be tried as adult. (for grand theft) auto. The total cost of these changes has not been calculated depending on what state you live in. Cost could run into the millions per state. The Legislative Fiscal bureau, has estimated that lowering the age at which people are treated as adults in criminal cases cound run into the thousand of dollor per case. Critics say, new bills could increase every person tax base (depending on what state you live in) which is not favorable to most people. These are radical change and radical feiws. But we all must face the fact. We must do something radical to change, or alter crime in our young, Before they become to big discipline.

Race of criminals - The second factor to determind who are the criminals would be race. Race is a very important element in determining who are the criminal reasons vary. Most cromologest beleve certain groups commited more crimes then other. In this section I will emphis the two major groups of people in the united state blacks and whites First blacks. Blacks in America make up 18% of the tottal population in the contry. around (10 million) Crime among the black commitys have stabled off over the past 30 years. Reason could be blacks are more involved in political power instead of voilence amoung one another. Blacks are starting to utilize there number to enforce change in there commitys Higher living standards have changed many blacks veiw about the white majorty. Crime is not a thing of the past for many. Blacks still commit more Criminal act then white (according to police data) Crime like burglart grand theft, shop lifting, homicides ect. Are still over represented by blacks. Aside from being usually male, the offenders are usually young and poor, and come from broken family. 25% of black males between the age of 16 to 24 are on probation in the united state. According to uniform Crime report. Black males also make up 42% of the total prison population in the united states, these figures can be altered. If black males between the ages of (16 and 24) change there attitudes toward society, and the astablishment and accept the statues que. (more about black on probation later)

Black Population of 50 metropolition Cities 2007

City	Black population	Total population
1. New York-	2,102,512	7,322,564
2. Chicago-	108,771	2,783,736
3. Detroit-	777,916	1,027,974
4. Philadelphia-	631,936	1,585,577
5. Los Angeles-	487,674	3,485,398
6. Houston-	457,990	1,630,553

7. Baltimore-	436,768	736,014
8. Washington DC-	399,604	606,900
9. Memphis-	334,737	610,337
10. New Orleans-	307,728	496,938
11. Dallas-	296,994	1,006,877
12. Atlanta-	264,262	394,014
13. Cleveland-	235,405	505,616
14. Milwaukee-	191,255	628,088
15. Birmingham-	168,277	265,968
16. Boston-	166,945	574,283
17. Indianapolis-	165,570	731,327
18. Jacksonville-	160,283	635,230
19. Columbus-	142,748	632,910
20. Cincinnati-	138,132	364,040
21. Kansas City-	128,768	435,546
22. St. Louis-	126,522	435,546
23. Charlotte-	125,827	395,934
24. Nashville-	118,627	488,374
25. Richmond-	112,122	203,054
26. San Diego-	104,261	1,110,599
27. Nor Folk-	102,012	261,229
28. Buffalo-	100,579	328,123
29. Miami-	98,207	358,598
30. Pittsburg-	95,362	369,879
31. Louisville-	79,783	269,063
32. San Francisco-	79,039	723,959
33. Dayton-	73,595	182,044
34. Rochester-	73,024	231,636

35.Oklahoma City-	71,064	444,719
36. Tampa FL.-	70,131	280,015
37. San Antonio-	65,884	935,935
38.Greensboro SC.-	62,305	183,521
39. Denver CO.-	60,046	467,610
40. Sacramento-	56,521	369,365
41. Hait Ford-	54,338	139,739
42. Seattle-	51,948	516,259
43. Phoenix-	51,053	983,403
44. Minneapolis-	47,648	368,383
45. Orlando-	44,303	164,693
46. Portland-	33,530	437,319
47. Province-	23,828	160,228
48. Albany-	20,869	101,082
49. Honolula-	4,821	365,272
50. Salt Lake City-	2,742	159,936

White Criminals- Criminal in the white race is feiw, but many The crime commit by the white Americans are very semilar to black Americans. Most crime commed by white are from the lower econmic groups. White with incomes of less then 10,000 yearly commit crime, such as burglery, larceny, and motor vehichal theft. White in higher income level around 50,000 or more commit crimes Insurance Fraud ect. Acording to police and the FBI data, white American are more proned to crime as they grow older. Reason cary but to most crimologest beleive white American change there feiw to society as they become more educated. White American are changing there out look yat live and starting to approach live more concred. The complexed society we lives in is started to effect white Americans. And in a country where everything is money, white American are starting To rethink how they veiw government, and the country as a whole.

Gender of crimnal - Males and Female.

Male make up 49% of the total population in the United States. But they account for 90% of vilent crimes listed in table 2 bottom

Offence	Male	Under 18	Under 21	Under 23	Black 49%
Criminal Homicide	88%	9%	24%	43%	48%
Forcible rape	99%	15%	31%	52%	60%
Aggravated Assault	93%	29%	51%	71%	37%
Arson	87%	14%	28%	47%	33%
Offence against family and children	89%	42%	31%	50%	21%
Weapons carrying posseing	89%	15%	55%	67%	36%
Percent of group in total population	49%	13-17%	15%	33%	37%

Percentage of those arrested falling into various social categories Excluding white, and blacks. But not including Indians, Chinse, Japan and all other Those age 12 and under hae been omitted from this caloulption because the percentage of arrests for this age group is extremely law source Figures calculated from Federal Bureau of Investigation uniform crime report 1990 Government printing office Washington DC. Social factors do predict to some extend which offenders will become chronic The most clear are sex, and age. Males are far more likely than females to become chronic delinquents, and the general rule for age is for lower age of the first police contact. The greater The number and the more serious. The offenses. Lower econimic males are more likely to become chronic delinquents, but the evidence is unclear According to most studys Male criminal engage in crime for varise reason, beside crime such as Auto theft, mugging homicide, weapons changes. Males cause law enforcement agency more problems then females.

Females criminals - Female criminal are on the raise, do to the change in women wule over the past 30 years. Crime such as shoplifting, child abuse, and countrebands are up By woman all threw the country. Although the criminal statistics continued in the FBIs uniform crime reports are somewhat limited in scope, especially for crimes involving women, they are the best available and can at least be accepted as an indicater of trends. During the decade from 1970 to 1980. The amount of female crime as indicated by arrests grew by only 39.1 percent. During the same period, male arrests grew by only 5.5 percent This dramatic difference can be seen in certain kind of crime in which women offenders have become more and more involved (and reported in the past ten years. Arrest figures for females, under eighteen years of age are especially note worthy compared to those for males of the same age group. The most dramatic increase were found in aggravated assault up to 106.5 percent and burglery up to 90.6 percent For males offenders under eighteen these crimes increased only 57.9 percent, and 29% percent respectively for the decade. Another interesting statistic comes from the arrests data for motor vehicle theif while arrests for males decreased by 27.3 percent, those for female shot up by 41 percent overall, violent crime arrests for all female offenders increased 55.5 percent, slightly more than the 40 percent increase reporting for men. It is in the property crimes where the increase overall is so dramatic for women 92.6 percent as compared to 31.5 percent for men. These figures clearly indicate the growing roles of the females offenders in the entire criminal justice system. One crime which women are over represented is crime in prostitution There is a estimated 500,000 prostitution can be one of at least three non-martial acts

(1)Engaging in sexual relations with another person for a fee, usually around25$ or less

(2)offering or (soliciting) to engage in sexual relationships with another person for a fee or something of value.

(3)requests, or agree to pay a fee or something of value to another person for sexual service and acts.

The fee, or something of value is most often money. Members of wither sex my now be convicted of prostitution as distinguished from the past when only women could be convicted Most states prostitution statues forbid prostitution by males selling sexual service to other males. Males who offer to pay a women to engage in sec acts may also be charged with the crime if the statutes of that jurisdiction apply to both sex. Efforts to decriminalize prostitution in the united states have met with little success. Only the state of Nevada, has legalized prostitution. In Nevada each county has The option as to whether prostitution will be legalized fifteen of Nevada's seventeen counties have decided to remove the legal restraints against prostitution. Many cities and states have ordinances and statutes that create the offence of loitering to solicit prostitution such laws do not require proof of prostitution, or solictation to commit prostitution but instead are addressed to street walkers who are loitering for the purpose of soliciting for prostitution. Prostutes (A) may operate Independently (B)under the control of a pimp (C)as a part of an orginized syndicate (D)with person other than the above. Prostitution is one crime which has been a problem to law enforcement agency sence law enforcement agency Have keep data on the crime. Prostitution will always be with us, unless we as people ecept the fact we are all sexual beings at birth. And as long as we have man and women. There will always be a market for prostitution.

Homeless people

A new bread of criminal which is emerging today is the homeless American. Homeless people such as drug attics, driveter, runaway ect The homeless population is growing in ever major city in the united state. no one knews why the homeless population is growing. Reason could be

(1)loss of jobs, do to change in technology

(2)devorce

(3)Drugs and alcohol abuse

(4)Demestic Violence

(5)Abuse - By family members

(6)Cut back on social programs

(7)Mental ill people what ever the reason.

Heres a breif veiw of Each

(1)<u>Loss of job-</u> Millions are losing there job, to competition over seas. A loss of job to any person brings stress, and heart ache with the stress bring ideas of criminal activites. Loss of job is the number one reason why people turn to crime. With unemployment rate the way they are today. Law enforcement agency are very aware of unemployed worker, who may turn to crime for muuntary gains, or for shelter.

(2)<u>Divorce -</u> Half of the marrige today end up in divorce within the first 5 years. High divorce rate leads to broken family and loss love one Divorce men and women end up on the street with no were to turn and no were to go. And with a combination of a job loss you can see why Homeless divorce people may conceder turning to crime and law enforcement agency are very aware of this fact.

<u>Drug and Alcohol abuse</u> - Drug and alcohol abuse is the number two cause of homelessness, besides job loss, and Divorce in this country. Million of American have substain abuse problem. Which leads to trouble on the job, and at home. Drug and alcohol abuse is a very big problem in the united state, compared to other country, Most alcohol, and drug attic who can not hold a job. End up on the street which lead them to a live of crime. Drug and alcohol abuse is a effecting every person in the country, and government most some up with new way of approaching This vast problem, (more about drug and alcohol later in the book,

<u>Demestic Vilence -</u> Demestic vilence cases are on the raise thewout the country. People seem to not be able to cope with one another. There is a lot of factor such as drug, alcoholism, disagrement between two parties ect Domestic violence seems to accompany social change in all countries In comparison with other countries. The unites states is

somewhere in the middle with regard to the total amount of violence experienced. Demestic vilence will contiue to encrease, unless people put aside there diffrence, and come up with a civilized way of handling disputes.

Abuse, by Family member - Family members are abused by their own loved one more so then with strangers. Demestic crime which lead to homelessness, is caused by a number of reason. The disturbance, or violence could include not only adults but also children within the family unit. Past experience has demunstrated that family trouble calls can be dangerous for law enforcment office Approximately one-fifth of police deaths, and almost one third of assaults on officers occur in responding to family Quarrels. study have shown abuse by family members is one of the most unreported crimes in the united states among the offenses, are

(1)homicides one-quarter to one third of all homicides are domestic murders in which one family member kills another.

(2)crimes against children child beating child neglect child abuse physical and sexual incest ect.

Crime against other members of the family abuse of parents by children abuse of the parent. Crime against family members is deep routed in our society. And must be confronted for the future.

Cut back on Social Programs - Social program are being cut in ever state in the union. Program which is put in place to help the needed are being taking away by state government, also at the federal level These cut backs are putting needed family on the street once on these street, these family turn to crime to fed themself. Social programs have to be restored if we are to have a country of productive members of society. Instead of a country of beggers. Social programs have been in place sence the new society program enacted during the resevelt adminstration of the 1930's. Millions of people need these program to live. And if we want people off the street, and back in housing. Government must restore program to help the down and out.

Mental Illness-Criminal - some people who have mental disorders are living on the street. State, and local government are cutting back on program to help the mental, Ill, sick people who need medical help are being turn away by family and friends. These pcople commit crime because They are on the street 90% of the time Crime such as petit theif, shoplifting pandering, are crime commited by the mential ILL. There are over 10 million mentally Ill people in the unites state. Ans with this amount of numbers, Community across the country, most come up with solution on how to soup with the mentally Ill criminal. Instead of placing then inside some institution, or rubber room, and threwing away the key.

Hate Groups - skin Heads milita Groups and the Klux Klux Klan are another group of criminal who are on the raise, today these group seem to be growing thew out the united state Groups of these kind have been around for decade. The rebirth of these groups come about when times get tough. Each of these group Have diffrent Prospective of how to deal with monoritys in the united states Here there prospectives of each group.

Skin Head - The skin head are a subcutural group which started in europe around the late 1970's there idealgy as the same as the Nazie party which was formed by Adolf Hitler in the late 1920's This group preaches hate of Jews, backs, and other minority in the united states. There are about 100,000 in number. And there avarage age between 18-24. They are mostly in the eastern and western state. And southern state in one state in particular (Alabama)

Militia Groups - Militia groups are on the raise by people who don't agree with the skin heads, or other hate groups. These groups main fuction is to surprass monority groups. Militia groups are located in the midwestern state, and the south east state There are about 500,000 members thewout the united state. There average age is about 20-40 years of age.

Klux, Klux, Klan - Started back in the mid 1800's There funtion then was to catch runaway slaves, and to keep blacks from voting in the south The Klan of the today is using more sofasticated means of spreading hate, know the group is working within state, and local Goverment. To surpress The growth of people of color within the political Ring. The Klan orgnization is mostly located in the souther state. The average age of Klan members are between 5-75 There are about 600,000 members threwout the south. American majority is tired of these subcutural groups, and want law enforcement agency to put these group out of business for good. Law enforcement agency want to surpress these groups by montering there movement threwout north america. To spreed hate of any group of people is wrong We as civilized being must come together to stop the spreed of Hate so we all can coexist on this small planted call earth.

The cost of Criminals

There is a cost in nearly everything in this live and the cost of crime is no diffrent. The cost of criminal activity To business Prison system and courts cost over 600 billion a year in our country In this section. I will place empasis on the cost of each each and want prison, and courts and business organization can keep these cost in lives. First cost of crime to business Despite soaring expenditures on private security devices like closed circuit television business across the country are loosing billions of dollars each years from such crime, as retail pilferage, and shop lifting bribery, kick backs, and fraud. The private sector of America currently spends 64 percent more on security measure alarms systems licks, guards. whit all the money business are putting in to protect there business, Criminals are still costing business billion internal losses, especially theft by employees and external losses especially shoplifting legally crimes

The Cost of Criminals

against business include several type of property crime larceny, arson, forgery, and counterfeiting, fraud, embezzlement, buying and selling stolen property, and vandalism. Although defined in public law, most crimes against business, are handled by private secirity. Ralatively few cases, are ever reported to public police relatively few are proscuted. Anti business criminal offenders come from a cross section of American society both sex and, all ages, and ethnic groups are included. The

28

two major loss to business are employee theift, and shoplifting. These two loss a long cost company over 200 billion dollars anually. Heres a endepth veiw of each.

Employee theift - According to a number of observers, theft by employees appears to be common widespread, and even acceptable. The theft may range from objects of minimal value such as stationary supplies to embezzlements that run into millions of dollars. One rough overall estimate is that 50 percent of the nations workforce engages in some sort of theift. Another observer see a better than 50% percent change to sizable dishonesty and a 25 percent change of costly malpractice in the average business The employee theift may wear a white collar, or blue collar He or she may be a manager, or high executive. In fact some of the most spectacular cases of theift by employees have involved executive The meaning of honesty, as it relatives to theft by employee becomes problematic if management expects its employees to steal Yet it would appear that this is often the case workers have long been accustomed to wages in kind, or extras to supplement their objective dollar, or material ernings. In this sense occupational theift can be tolerates as an informal type of fringe benefit One study of managers that such unofficial rewards such as promotions are Quicker, and more convenient to dispense than more formal rewards such as promoting. For crimes against business it tis personal advantage that is clearly involved The individual benefits, and the business loses. The most common reason for tolerance of stealing from large businesses was that large business can aford it. The truth of the matter is, large business cannot aford it. with ever loss to business large or small. The cost is retured to the consumer in higher prices. Higher prices is then returned to us all. In less Quality products. The solution to employee theift is not higher wages, shorter work hour early returment ect. Employee must learn to Exept the business is being part of there own. If employee feel the buiness is there, (or a part of it) They will not steal from the orgnization, and will have more import into the company. There more been recent attempt to discover whether. Certain type of people are more likely than other to be involved in theft from their employers. Those employee between the ages of 16 to

21 were more likely than older employees 24 to 65 to have committed an act of employee theift Aside from age, sex also made a difference 60% percent of males compared with 43 percent of females were above the middle point on an employee deviance, Also employees with less seniority, those working fewer hours, and those dissatisfied with work, and promotional opportunites were also more likely to be involved in employee theft. On the other hand, level of education, type of firm rate of pay, whether or not the employee was a supervisor, and how management dealt with deviance made little difference in employees involvement. The study also focused on sex as a variable of dishonest employees, who were involved in the theift of cash, merchendise or both found that males committed more theft than females. 40 percent of the employees but 56 percent of the violator were male. Males were also more likely to commit theifts involving more money. The study showed that younger employees ages (18 to 22) were most likely to steal on the other hand, older women 41 and over were more likely to steal than older men. The rate of theft was higher in jobs charcteized by sex stereotyping. In particular, women who stole were usually in clerical and sales positions The study was a very comprehensive one of thefts by employee in retail store, manufacturing firms, and hospitals. Regarding offenders characteristics, these researchers found higher levels of theft by

(1) Younger, and never married employees-

(2) Employees who had both an opportunity to steal and knowlege about.

(3) things to be taken.

(3) Employee who were concerned with improving themelves and with.

(4) metting career goals.

(5) Disatisifed employees especially younger one

The most consistent predictor of theft was the employees perceived chance of being caught.

However, informal sanctions by coworkers appeared to ne about twice as Influential in shaping behavior as the more formal responses of management sex as a variable also needs some Qualification. While it is true that male employees are more likely than females to be involved in theift Most males employee would not teal from there employers if they hade more say or impute in important desition conserning the company. To sum up some what in contrast to business crime offenses against organization revolve around well-defined criminal acts. From the estimates available, it would appear that only a small fraction of the offenses which occur are ever reported to the police or prosected in the public legal ystem. Thus, crimes against business, even though they are liolations of substantive criminal law, are usually handled outside the criminal justice system.

<u>Shoplifting</u> - The second biggest to business is the crime of shoplifting which can be defined as theft from a retail tore by people who pose as legitimate customers of the store. For crime reporting purposes, shoplifting is treated as a type of larceny-theft. As it turns out, about 11 percent of reported larcenies are for shoplifting currently seen in American society to begin with the United states is a consumer society Materialistic values are held by large number of people. Shoplifting has been studied more often than theft by employee, however, most studies have attempted to charactize shoplifting. In general such an approach may be musleading for the one reason frequency of arrests as, well as age, and sex of offender may variation from store to store. For another, shoplifting may be common to all groups, but store personal may be instucted to watch for a particular group, such as juvenile. Juveniles have the highest theift rate reported by police.

<u>Shoplifters by Gender</u> - Men and women, and race, black and white

<u>Men shoplifter</u> - Men shoplifter are oun the raise in hundreds of community thewout north America. Traditial and women profesion, male are seeing the opounity as being very profoatable. The average age of male shoplifter are between the age 19 and 25, after age 25 shoplifting by male levels off. According to many, sources shoplifting is becoming a big business To male. With prophet eceding into the

billion dollor yearly Business will have to come up with new ideas to curtail this new boom by male.

Women shoplifters - The involvement of women in shoplifting has long been known, and some sociologists have argued that shoplifting is basically an extension of the woman role as family shopper, However, this appears to be changing as American women approach equality with there male counter parts. During the 1970 and 1980' arrest rates of female for theft arrests are for shoplifting To say that shoplifting by females has increased is not to say that shoplifting is a uniquely female crime. It is worth noting that about 70 percent of larceny arrests are arrests of males. The average age by most women are between 20 and 35. After age 35 women shoplifting levels off, for women.

Black Shoplifters - black shoplifter accounted for a high degree of los to business threwout many communitys. According to many survey, Blacks shoplifted two times as much then whites. Black females accounted for the majority of the theifts. (According to police data) The average age of black female, who commited these theif. Are between the age of 18 to 22. Most of the theift occur in southern state, where there i a high degree of black female population.

White Shoplifters - White shoplifters account for billions of dollors To losses to business. Most shoplifters are white females between the age of 16 and 20. Most of the theifs orvcur in large metroplotian area. Business organization themelves do not know the exact amount of money they lose to crime. Most industries attempt to calculate an inventory shrinkage figure, which is estimated to be somewhere between 2 and 6 percent - for some store, up to 9 or 10 percent - of the total inventory depending upon the nature clerical, and billing error, much of it may be attributable to crime. If 2 or 3 percent sound like a small amount. It must be realized that annual sales of the Fortune 500 corportion along exceed 1 trillion Hence shrinkages victimization for robbery, and burglary are related to both type and size of business wholesale businesses have the highest rate of burglary vicimizations, and service business the lowest rates for robbery it is clearly retail businesses that are most likely to be affected, business victimization rates for burglary, and robbery increase as business get larger, but only up to a certain point, for burglary The rate starts to decline with businesses that have 1 million or more in receipt, also rate start to decline when the 500,000 level i reached.

Estimate Rate per 100,000 by business victimization by tyrect

business and victimization United State

Type of business	Base	Business Victimization	Burglary rate	Robbery rate
Total business	7,245,657	25,579	21,733	3846
Retail total	2,381,412	35,893	28,303	7590
Wholesale total	5,05,085	33,351	31,312	2040
Realestate	285,786	=	=	=
Service	367,539	=	=	=
Manufacturing	367,539	23,696	21,806	
Banks	69,961	-	-	-
Transportation	117,612	-	-	-
All other	721,933	14,251	12,838	1414

Criminal Justice system US Department of Justice 1998

As mention early, business with sale over 1 million in business suffer less losses, Also depending on location, city, and orgnization size.

The Cost of criminal To the Criminal Justice system courts

The cost of criminal to the criminal justice system, has gotten tottal out of control with lawyer fee running rappet. With criminal activity going higher each year. The cost to the criminal Justice system is sky rocketing. In this section we will look at the criminal justice system as, a whole, The beginning of the court system, The probation system. Also we will look at the prison system today. And how the prison system has changed, and were it will be in the future.

Court system - The criminal justice system is a 100 trillion dollar a year industry. The complexed system of the courts. Varies from state to state. And from community to community. The criminal court ascat the core of the American criminal justice system. The courts are highly structured, deeply venerated, and circumscribed by law and tradition. The rest of the system is dependent upon, and responsible to the courts. The criminal justice system is composed of three separate subsystems, police courts, and jail (corrections)- Any more ased success by the police impacts on courts, and jail by overloading already heavy work schedules also if corrections cannot succeed in its reintegration efforts The police are overloaded with report offenders. Individual rights has clearly been the goal of the courts quiet but effective revolution. The decisions of the much-maligned-or revered warren courts are more readily understood when viewed from this perspective, During the 1960's nearly all the guarantees of the fourth, fifth, sixth, and eight Amendments of the constitution were made binding on the states The Fourteeth Amendment provided the primary leverage in this landmark decision, (Nute) These desion have been wrote about before in other text. (1)Mapp vs Ohio exclusion rule The case Mapp vs Ohio 367.us 643 1960 Dealt with illegal obtaining of evedence. Its primary intersity here lies in the courts use of the Fourteeth Amendment to support its decision. (2)In the California case of Robinson vs California cruel, and unusual Punishment 370 us 660 1961 the Eighth Amendmend clause forbiding cruel, and unusual punishment was made binding on state proceedings. The case involved the arrest of a subject on the charge of being a drug addicts, even thought he had neither used drugs in the state that law that imprison a person for being sick inflicts a cruel, and unusual punishment inviolation of the Eighth Amendment, and due proccess under the fourteenth Amendment

Gideon v wainwright In the crucial decision of Gideon v Wainwright 372 us 335 (1963) the court held the defendants in a noncapital case are entitled to asistance of counsel at trial as a mater of right This right was extended to state proceeding again under the provision of the Fourteeth Amendment. These cases don't have to be discused in great length. The 14 Amendment has changed the court system in all 50 states. If you need moor information on 14th Amendment, check your library in your city, or community. There should be books on this landmark Amendment.

Today criminal courts process offender though a complex series of steps from initial appearance to sentence. Each step allows for charges to be dropped, or cases to be dismissed Many of the stages, especially the later ones allow for judges, prosecutors, and defense attorney to enter into negotiations over the charge, or the sentence it is in the interpretation of the history, and present-day function. of criminal courts that the difference among the major perspectives become apparent. A due process view of the courts calls attention to the constitutional guarantees of offenders rights From this perspective, the extension of constitutional rights to offenders in state criminal cases represents a most positive development, such as (Gideon v Wainwright) or (Escobedo v ILLINOIS) which erved to protect defendants right against self incrimination, can be cited as hallmarks of a trend toward fairness, and equity in criminal court procedure:

(1)<u>Initial appearance</u> - After arrest a suspect is finger printed photography and advised of the right to remain silent and the right to counsel.

(2)<u>Preliminary Hearing</u> - After the initial appearance, the accused is giving a preliminary hearing which is a judicial examination to determine probable cause for belief that a crime has been committed.

(3)<u>Bail, or Detention</u> - Also after the initial appearance, the accused is taken before a judicial authority for a civil hearing.

(4)<u>Grand Jury Indietment</u> In this stage, the grand jury hears the evidence developed by the prosecutor. If it agrees that prosecutions is warranted, a true bill or indictment declaring that the suspect should be tried is returned. If the grand jury does not agree Ie refuses to indict = the prosecutor may still file an information which is roughly equivalent to an indictment.

Arraignment - At the arraignment, the indicated suspect appears before a judge. After hearing the changes the suspect may pled guilty, or not guilty.

Trail - In the trial, evidence is presented, and challenged both by the prosecution, and by the defense on the basis of the evidence a verdict of guilty, or not guilty is reached.

Right to speedy Trial as a defense - (The sixth Amendment)

of the US constitution provides that in all criminal prosecutions the accused shall enjoy the right to a speedy, and public. Trail Most defendants charged with serious crime do not ordinarily wish eigher a speedy trail is waived with the consent of the trail court, the constitutional mandate of a speedy trial must be complied with Some states have enacted staturing requriements that specify the time period in which a defendant must be tried These statutes do not necessarily incorporate constitutional standards, and may use alternate remedies without violations the sixth Amendment requirement. In holding that right to a speedy trail commences when a person is indicted arrested, or other wish officially accused.

Sentenceing - At a separate hearing the convicted defendant is sentenced. In sentencing a number of alternatives are available to the court based on the statute in a given state.

This was only a breif reveiw of a outline of the court systems for criminal. Going threw this mase of the criminal justice system is very compled, and confesing. This is were the court system in the unites states needed to be simplued. Proseters, Public defendents judges, all agree. The system has loophole, and can be improved. This outline very from state to state and city to city, also depending on were you live. This outline may vary.

Plea bargan, Appeals, probation, Prison, Parol, The second phases of the court system in united state is based upon the plea bargain threw the parole systems. In this section we will look at these imporant aspects of criminal. Justice system, and The importants of all 5 to criminal.

Plea bargain - Basically a plea bargain is the defendants agreement to plea guilty to a criminal charge with the reasonable expectaion of receiving some considcration from the state Five major types of plea bargains have been distinguished (1)judicial participation and indication of the sentence (2) modification of changes by the prosecutor (3) prosecutorial agreement to make sentencing recommendations (4) type 2 and type 3 combined (5) type 1 and 2 combined in terms of charge, the plea bargain may involve horizontail charge reduction, in which a defendant pick one, two or three out of many similar chargers, and please guilty only to those, or vertioal change reduction in which a defendant pleas guilty to a less serious charge. Since much plea bargaining occurs within the judicial system and remains Hidden from public view, it is difficult to quantify the case falling into each type of bargaining However, there is little doubt that plea bargaining is far more common than trails are in virually all jurisdictions of the United States It is interesting to note that plea bargaining i by no means a recent phenomenon. This consepts has been, used for hundreds of years. And hundreds of criminal have used this concept to get sentence reduced from felony to misdemeans. Never th less, dispite its prevalence, and historical basis, bargaining justice continues to be regarded with suspicion Certainly, bargaining justice is contrary to the nation of due precess The constitutional right to a fair trial is given up The negative aspects of plea bargaining should not be allowed to obscure its positive functions, which perhaps explain why it continues dispite strong disapproval by many.

Appeal - Another phase of the court system is the appeal process The entire process steams of course, from a conviction of guilt by some court system at the municipal, county, state, or federal level In each case. These appeals, know as postconviction remedies were not generally available untill the last 100 years or so. They are usually made by the defendant. The state is unlikely to appeal a decision, regardless of the out come if the accused is convicted, that is the result the state was after, and if the accused is declared innocent, the state cannot appeal - The constitution guarantees that someone who is found innocent cannot be placed in double. The effects of an appropiately introduced appeal is a stay in the execition of the original sentence until the appeal is decided, As soon as possible, If not immediately after the sentence is pronounced, The defendants counsel must either move for a new trial, or make an appeal on some reasonable ground since appeal courts usually make short work of foiolouis appeal But as long ago as the 1930' significance of the appeal process was firmly established.

The courts Appeal - Appeal of each state, by level immediately above the trial court is usually called the court of appeals. In some states, and in federal system, there is more than one level of appeal. In these cases the highest level of appeal to court is generally called a supreme court. The supreme court of the united states is the court of last resort.

(state court system)	(federal court system)
(Level 4) supreme court of criminal appeal supreme judicial court ect	Court of last resort. US supreme court.
(Level 3) Intermediate Apellate court District court Superior court of appeal ect.	Intermediate appealate US court of appeals
(Level 2)Trial courts Courts of state general jurisdiction circuit court District court state court county court	Trial courts US District courts
lower court justice of the peace small claims court Traffic courts Magistrates Courts ect	US magistates and specialized courts 98% success rate.

(Note)

Paralle, i between state court ystems, And the Federal Court appeal court focus is a intermediam, between the two depending on were you live this graph may vary. The US supreme court will usually hear cases from the state system only after the defendant has exhausted all state remedies, and the case has been finally adjudicated. In most state systems, the court of appeals reviews the decisions of most trial court for judicial error. The fact in a case are not in question, and the trial courts decisions on that aspect of case are binding on the appellate court because of this aspect of appellate review, evidence on the facts of the case is not presented to the court of appeals rather, review is based on the trial record, An appellate court cannot reverse the factual findings of the trial court unless they are totally erruneous. in states where there is a second level of review, the trial record, and the intermediary courts decisions are examined. Usually the refusal to hear an appeal over a lower appellate courts ruling is the same as upholding the decision and the case stops there, unless an appeal is filed separately in a federal court of appeals on some constitutional The federal court system currently includes ninety-one trial courts federal district courts and eleven intermediary review courts counts of appeal between the state trial courts, and the country in eleven circuits to facilitate servicing the ninety-one trial courts. Federal courts are restricted in their power. The federal courts of appeals are very similar to the state courts of appeal in that they review for error The cases tried by the federal district courts. In the early twentieth century, most appeals were based on the issues in the trial In the 1960's appeals began to move towards issues related to idividual rights under the us constitution using the fourteeth amendment as a lever, the supreme Court affirmend these rights to individuals in the separate states on a piecemeal basis under the hands off doctrine established by cheif Justice Felix Frankfurter, the court had restricted its early decisions to the actions of judges Later, abandoning the frankfurter policy, the court begin to impose procedural guidelines on law enforcement corrections, and every other element of the criminal justice system Constitutional right of prisons were more sharply defined by decisions of the appellate courts many of these appeals came from desperate people behind prison walls. The criminal have been forced to become almost administative in nature because of the vast overload of cases. Since as many as 90% of trial conviction are appealed the review courts are equally in undated. The national advisory Commission on Criminal Justice standard and Goals expended a great deal of effort in trying to find way to reduce the court case load. The first recommendations that were made included in a number of alternatives.

<u>Screening</u> - one of the methods suggested was to place more stress on screening the basic guidelines for screening offenders vary greatly from Jurisdiction to help in developing fundamental criteria from screening suspected offenders out of the process Commity leaders have suggestions this plan to cut there heavg case loaded In most community this Has worked Screening Consisted of these basic functions.

An accused should be screened out of the criminal Justice system if there is not a reasonable likelihood that the evidence admissible against him would be sufficient to obtain a convition and sustain it on appeal. An accused should be screened out of the criminal justice system when the benefits to be derived from prosecution, or diversion would be out weighted by the cost of such action. Among the factors to be concidered in making this determination are the following

(1)any doubt as to the accused's guilt

The impact of further proceedings upon the accused and these close to him especially the likelihood, and seriousness of finanical hardship family life disruption

(3)The value of further proceedings in preventing future offences by other persons, considering the extent to which subjecting the accused to further proceedings could be expected to have an impact upon others who might commit such offenses, as well as the seriousness of these offenses.

(4)The value of further proceedings in preventing future offenses by the offender, in light of the offenders commitment to criminal activity as a way of life the seriousness of his past criminal activity which he might be reasonably be expected to continue The possibility that further proceedings might have a tendency to create, or reinforce commitment on the part of the accused to criminal activity as a way of life and the likelihood that programs available as diversion, or sentencing alternatives may reduce the likelihood of future criminal activity.

(5)The value of further proceeding in fostering the communitys sense of security, and confidence in the criminal justice system.

(6) The direct cost of prosecution, in terms of prosectorial time, court time, and similar factors.

(7) Any improper motives of the complainant.

(8) Prolonged nonenforcement of statute on which the charge is based

(9) The likelihood of prosecution, and conviction of the offender by another jurisdiction, and the like.

(10) Any assistance rendered by the accused in apprehension, or conviction of other offenders, in the prevention of offenses by other, in the reduction of the impact of offenses committed by himself, or others upon the victims, and any other socially beneficial activity engaged in by the accused that might be encouraged in others by not prosecuting the offender.

Diversion - A second major effort in the drive to reduce the number of cases brought to trial involves the diversion of offenders before conviction Diversion is quite different from screening it assumes that the individual will participate in some treatment program in return for removel from the criminal justice process before trial. In screening, the individual is dropped out of the process before it really begins, with no threat of continued prosecution, or promise of special programs for his, or her cooperation Diversion programs may be run by agencies with the criminal justice system, or by private, and public agencies entirely outside it. The primary benifit from both screening, and diversion programs is the ability to offer services to offenders without placing the stigma of further criminalization on them over criminalization usually a result of too many antiquated laws remaining on the books, is one of the reasons so many cases sit on dockets. The commissions also suggested guidelines for when diversion should take place. Diversion programs are another recognition of the situational nature of many crimes by expanding the base of available service, and keeping the offender cut of the damaging stages of the criminal justice process society gives the offender a much better charge to adjust in the community Diversion program, and Screening program has help thousands of criminal reajust to live outside In society without these program. The court system could not abstain the large values of case. These program will be around for many years to come. And hopefully these program will help crimial stay out of trouble in There commuity were they live.

Court based on raise, and Gender, and age

There has always been a saying that the legal system is blind when it come to raise, or Gender. This may be true in most cases, or is it In this section we will look at, The court system, and how blacks criminal, are treated over white criminal, and women criminal over men in America courts. First blacks criminal, over white criminal Blacks in the criminal Justice system Have long been discriminated against Depend who and were they live. There have been a number of studys From all regions of the country concerning black sentencing Depending on the crime, and There econmic backgrounds and age for instance young blacks Male(20-24) who commit crime such as Robbery, rape, larceny. Reserve 10% longer sentence Then younger white males If they live in southern state and western state. If older black males between the age of 30 to 60 Commit the same Crime in southern, and western state. There sentence were uslly reduced, by 10 years. Blacks who commited more harser crimes such as murder In southern state, and wester state, Reserve the death penalty 5 times as much as white, blacks who murder whites, in southern state and western state reserve the death peantly 43 percent more that whites who kill whites. Study of black young males between the age of 20 to 24 who live in northern state and eastern state who commited crimes such as rape, robbery, larceny burgery ect Reserve the same lenth of time for those crimes then whites. Older black males between the age of 30 to 60 who commit crimes like rape, robbery, larceny burgrely, ect, In northern state and in eastern state. reserve the same length of time Then white for the same crime. Blacks who commited homiceds in norther state and eastern state. Reserve the same lenth of time then whites. In short, there is soe descrimonation in the court system, depending on where you live, and the crime commited. And blacks males who are poor and live in states where there is clear out bias, are more likly to be subject to discrimation in the court system. This is also true for black female who commited crime in the states.

White Criminals - White crimianl in the court system who commited crime are more likly to reserve lighter sentence, for crime such as burglar, Robbery, rape ect If they live in southern state, and eastern state. For white criminal who live in northern state, and western state who commited The same crime resve 5 times shorter sentence then white who live in southern state and eastern state. Most of these satistic are based on white male between age of 20 to 24 white male between the age of 25 to 60 who commited crime such as larceny, grand theift burgary ect, reserve 10 time longer sentence in southern state and north state. Eastern state, and western state lessen ther sentence for the same crime. White male who commited crime such as homiceds reserve light sentence in norther state, and eastern state and rarley If ever reserve The Death peanlty for homicede cases In those state. White males comitted Homcide 5 times less then black male, and reserve less time for the same crimes.

Female White between the ages of 18 to 24 resve lighter sentence for crime such as theift Robbery ect In norther state and eastern state. But resved more lenther sentence for crime such as prostution and shoplifting IN nothern state and easter state. White female who commited those same crime between age or 18 to 24 reserve more lenther sentence In western state and in souther state. White female who commited Homiceds in the north, and east. Reserve less times on average 10 to 15 years less then white males, and black males and black females. White female who commited those same crime prositition, and shoplifting ect Reserve less time in southern state, and wester state. Older white female who commited crime such as shoplifting robbery ect, resve less time In all 50 state. Compared to all other genters. White female between The age of 25 to 60 who are convicted of the crime of child beating (a women crime) reseve less time usally - probation. Then black Female in the same age group, who also commited that same crime. In all 50 state. All in all white female seem to get lesser sentencing in all crime. Across the board. Compared to all other gender and age group

Black female - black female are part of the criminal Justice System Black Female between the age og 18 to 24 Commited more crime then white female in that same age groups. Crime mostly commited by black female are shoplifting, burgary, and prositition and illegal Drugs. When Convgted of these crime Black female send 5 times more jail time, or longer probation peroid then white females In southern state and western end states. If confegted of the same crimes In northern and eastern states. Black females who commited serious crimes such as a homicedin sothern state or western state reseve the depth peantly 2 to 1 over white female, in the same age group. But is black female commited crime in the north or east. There prison terms (usually live) is reduced to 20 years or less Black female between the age of 25 to 60 who commited crime such as shoplifting, prositution illegal drugs ect. In northern state and western state. Reseve finds. and almost all the time never spend any jail time. Black female who commited these crimes in eastern stare and southern state may have to spend some jail time for these crimes. All in all Depending on the Juge, the location the city and state. Black Females along with the rest of the genders. Have to deal with a court system which is very complexed and feeled with a diversity group of people who make the desition on other people live. Ans the desitition they make meaning Juges and Jury effect people from all walks of live. And Depending on what state city, or commited your live in. The desition they make will vary from judge to judge, from city to city state to state.

Probation-Parole-Prison - The next lenk of the American Justice system is the system of probation, Parole and prisons. In this section we will look at each one And do they work for the criminal or against them first Probation.

Probation - FFollowing a determination of guilt, or incent the courts have a number of options for dealing with offenders. In recent times the option most often selected is probation Probation is a derivate of the suspended sentence handed down to us some what indirectly by way of post judicial procedures. Both suspended sentence, and probation involve mitigation of punishment for an offender throught a judicial procedure. The suspended sentence differs from probation thought the terms are sometimes used interchangeable. The suspended sentence does not require supervision, and usually does not prescrible a specified set of goals for the offender to work towards. It is merely a form of quasifreedom that can be revoked, with a prison sentence imposed at the instruction of the court. Sentence can be suspended in two ways

(1) The sentence is imposed, but executions of it is suspended

(2) Both the imposition, and execution of the sentence are suspended of these two, the second is the more desirable because of reduced stigma However, the practice of suspending sentences, like sanctuary, has generally been replaced with suspervise probation in America Sentences may be vacated by the sentencing judge, and the offenders may be placed at liberty in the community. But this is a relatively infrequent occurrence. Across the nation, probation is administered by hundreds of seprate agencies with a wide variety of rules, and structures within the states, while one agency may be required to serve juvenile, misdemeanant, and felony offenders, another agency may handle only one type of offender The term probation has multiply meanings within the multiple areas of correction. As (1) a <u>dispossition</u>, probation was first seen as a new type of suspended sentence. If convicted offenders could meet certain conditions established by the court they were allowed to remain in their comminuties under limited freedom. These conditions vary usually included prohibitions regarding drinking and travel and association with undersitable persons curiently, probation is used as a sentence in it own right. As (2) a <u>status</u> probation has many advantages for offenders while their freedom is some what limited their status is considered better than that of confined offenders They are neither completely free nor totally restricted they can work, keep their family together avoid stigma of incarceration, andmake restitution to their victims as (3) a <u>subsystem</u> of the criminal justice system, probations has many different stuctures, and organizations In this context it refers to the adminstratives agency that provides the probation services that probation performs for its administrative agency that provides the probation service to juvenile or adult offenders. The set of

functions, activites, and services that probation performs for its administrative agency and the offender is the probation process. The process model for probation service is usually seen as a series of interlinking activites between the courts the offender, and the offenders community and its resources.

The process includes the offenders reporting regularly to a probation officer the servicing of the offenders needs through treatment counseling and so on, and the officer supervision of the probationer to ensure that the rules of the probation order are observed. So probation todayis a process that provides the judge with an alternative disposition that results in an improved satus for the offenders within a subsystem of the criminal justice system knowledge of the multiple meanings of probation will generate a through understanding of probation today.

Probation based on rase, age, Gender, Location-

Probation based on race - Black American Men

The probation system in the united state is over represented by males. Most of these male are young black men, between the age of 18 To 24. Compared to White males. Most of these young offender are located in southern state. Young black males over represented any other group of people white male, white female, black female, ect when it comes to probation. Many of these young men are poor, and come from broken family. Poobation for these individual gives them a second change to improve. As citizen instead of Incarcaration. Most Liberal agree. Probation can serve as a key stone to a second change for many who have feeled in society which is complicated, and bias, And at time unjustifibly wrong to sertain group pf people.

White Males in the Probation system - White male who are in the probation system is represented by a sertain percentage. Most of these white males are young between the age of 20 To 24 The majority of these males who are own probation are located in western state. One state in particular. Which has the largest amount of white male on probation is the state of California. California has over 100,000 white males on probation according to FBI Data Governer pronal suornager

Policys to fight crime by any means. Is working acording to satistic Crime is down in that state do to antic criminal leslation Past by state legistaters All other western state white male on probation is to small to of a percentage to elabarate.

Black female - black female who are infolved with the probation system are usually young (age 20-25) most of them who are on probation are located in southern state. Know one knows the exact amount of blacks females who are on probation in those state Acording to many, there are over 1 million between four state, George, Flordia, NorthCarlona, South Carlona.

White Female - White female who are Involved in probation are mostly located In western state, Once again, they are uslly young women between the age of 19-25. White female make up The lesser amount of people our probation. Then any other gender. All other gender of nationalty Asia American, Portricas American ect Make up around 500,000 In all 50 state combined.

Prison system - Prison are complexed social orginization. They are closed communities generally unisexual, and relatively homogeneous in term of age, that attempt to maintain total social control would be possible if inmates were willing to submit to it. In this section we will look at the prison system in the united state How the system beginning, Prison treand, Black prisoners over white female prisoner.

The beginning of the prison system - When you look at the beginning of the prison system, you must first look at the history of prison In the united state. The prison system began round the early 1800 Two important new models apeared pretaining two prison

(1) The Auburn model, first established at the Auburn state prison in New York between 1819 and 1823 prisoners slept alone in their cells at night, and labored together in workshops during the day

(2) The pennsylvania model reflecting a quaker influence, began in 1826 in pittsburgh, and 1829 in Philadelphia. It isolated conviots for the entire period of their confinement, required them to maintain silence,

and made them work along in their cells Although there were intense debates between advocates of the two models, both were dependent upon isolation of prisoners from the community and establishment of a disciplined routine. Regimentation became the standard mode of prison life. This change in the dominant mode of corrections - from coporal punishment, or the mechanisms of shame to imprisonment-is so sundamental that a more complete explanation is in order.

Post civil war Prison - The sixteenstates that built prisons between 1870, and 1900 were almost all in the northern, or western part of the country. Their only claim to improvement was the introduction of plumbing, and running water all were of the Auburn type, and the only modification in the older prison routine were the abandonment of the silent system, and the use of the interminate sentence, and pardle. In the south devastated by civil war, the penitentiary system had been virtually wiped out some state attempted to solve their prison problems by leasing out their entire convict population to contractors others took in convact work, or devise combination of both leasing out prisoners, and taking in contracts. The freed blacks were thus replaced by yet another group of slaves the convicted felons The south was unique in that it ignored the Auburn, and reformatory system The south's a grain economy.

The twentieth Century Industal Prison - from the begining of the twentieth century untill 1935. the number of inmate in united tates prison increase by 140 percent Ten new Auburn-stye prisons, and one based on Benthams Panopticon were built during this period-of ten referred to as the industrial era for prisons in America-which reached its zenith in 1935 These new prisons were considered as cold, and hard and abnormal as the prisoners whoms they were intended to persuade toward better things.

The Period of Transition - The Quarter century between 1935 and 1960 was one of the great turmoil within the prisons. Adminstrators, struck with the huge fortresses of the previous century were now deprived of the ability to provide meaningful work for inmates. The depression, and the criminal excesses of the 1920's and 30's hardened the public attitude toward convict. rebabilitation at a time when behavioral scientists were just beginning to propose hopeful reforms in pisoners treatment 5 Edger Hoover led the battle against the school of criminology His war on crime helped to give the world the super-maximum prison Alcatraz Located on an island in San Francisco bay, Alcatraz was constructed to house the hardest criminals in America when it was built in 1934 it was seen as the answer to the outrages of such desperate criminals as John Dillinger Bonnie, and Clyde, and Mabarker Eventually the US Bureau of prisons abandoned this idea as another failure, and Alcatraz was closed in 1963 Early efforts toward diagnastic classification, and case work were between 1915 and 1920 Edger Dolland W G Ellis in New Jersey in 1925 and an stearns in Massachusetts in 1930 Sanford Bates introduced these procedures into the US bureau of prisons in 1934 while sometimes borrowing principal from states across the nations, the US Bureau of Prisons gradully emerged as the national leaders in corrections, introducing mandy new concepts that have been copied by state systems Two major contributions were diagnosis and classification, and the use of professional such as psychiatrists and psychologists to help rehabilitate inmates. The federall system also led the way to more humane treatment and better living conditions But no matter how they were cleaned up, prisons remained monuments to idleness, monotony, frustration, and repression Despite attempts to tear down the massive walls around some prisons, the force of lock psychosis continued to hold out Prison inmates were feared as the convict bogey which could be dealt with only by lockeing and relocking counting and recounting.

The modern era of the prison system - The modern era of prison began about 1960 and it followed the pattrn of change that was to highlight the next decade. The 1960's in the United States were noted for tax bulent, and violent confrontations at almost every level of activity affecting human rights. The forces for change at work in the over all society were reflected in great pressure for change in corrections, ,as well. The drastic reinteipretations of criminal law, the civil right movement violent, and nonviolent domonstrations in the streets the assassinatios of popular president, and two other important natioal figures the

49

longest and most unpopular war in American history-all these outside presures were also felt inside the walls of the nations prison Reactions took the form of periodic violent prisons riots, and disorder. The supreme Court of the United States emerged as the primary external agent for the enforcced recognition of the basic right of those swept up in the criminal Justice system. This external pressure was generated by a long series of signigicant judicial interpretations. Finally, leadership and funding by the federal gevernment were provided to corrections administrators, and planners at the state, and local levels enabling them to create, implement, and evaluate new policies, and practices The impetus for change continues to the present day.

Prisons based on males and Females - Males have historically and overwhelmingly predominated the prison population although the number of sentenced prison is increasing rapidly over 95 percent of the total number of inmates in prison are males In corrections, as in the over all criminal Justice system women tend to receive more favorable disposition at ach major decision point in the system. This account, in part, for the over representations of men in prisons. Although crimes committed by women account for one out of every six arrests in America, less than one out of every thirty female offenders ends up in prison.

Black Males In the prison system - Young black (age 20-24) makes up a large portion f the prison enruolement. Most of these black males are young, and mostly located in the south Prison in the south are changing Do to presure from outside the area. groups such as the NaAcp, and other. Want more reform in southern prison. Do to the high number of blacks located in these prison. Reform for more human rights, and better treatment all around town blacks Is one issue which souther prison will have to deal with in the future.

White Males in the prison system - White males outnumber blacks in the nations jails nearly 11 out of 100 white male are Incarcerated Most white male who are in prison are located in the west. The averge age of most white males who are in the prison Is between 20 To 25.

Black Females In prison system - As stated earlyer, black females in the prison system are usually young. Average age 19-24 Most black female who are involved in the prison system are located In the south. Blacck female in souther prison make up 60% of female Population 6 out of 10 compared to the white conterparts

(white female)- White female involved in the prison system are mostly located in western state. Average age of most white female are 20 To 25. White female account for less population at prisons Then any other gender,

Alternative for the future - The prisons in the united state are over crowed and outdated - it will take billions of dollors and over 100 years to update, and change, the the current system in all 50 state. The changes will have to come at all levels of government state, local, federal, If these hange are not made by all level of goverment the prison system will see more attios, in the very near future. I suggest these change for the prison in the prison insutition

(1) more freedom of movement-for inmates within the prison walls

(2) less over ccrowed In state and Federal Prisons

(3) more freedom of speech How things should be ran within the system

(4) less sensership of prisoner mail prisoner calls ect

More freedom of movement - every one wants there freedom to move around even in prison Prisoners are still human beings. even those they may have committed a crime freedom of movement is one Issue most prisoner complane about will being in prison Being able to come and go within the prison walls Is one issue state and federal (1)prison will have to deal with in all 50 state.

less overcrowed In state, and Federal Prison.

Crowedness is a problem in all prison system (State and Federal) There more people today in the prison system then ever before. And with more people expected to enter ther prison system In the future Crowedness will be a problem, well into the next century. Everyone desereve to have a little peice in there lives (even prisoners) By giving each prisoner a bed a cell a peice, will give prisoner the privacy they disperatly need. This may not be a issure in all state and federal prison Some prison have a ell and a bed for prisner. Depending on location.

More freedom of speech on how things should be ran within The system. Prisner should have more say on how the system should be ran. After all they may be living there for a long time. Prisner should have more imput on when visteng Hour should be. What meals they want from day to day. Workout Hour ect. The freedom to choose what they want and when is vital To keep prisner less ideal Silver libertiys agee. Prisner need To Have more freedom in prison. To make simple desition such as, when light should go out, and what time to wake up.

Less sensership of prisner mail phone calls ect. Sensership of Prisners privancy is a problem in most prison Prisner want to have more privacy when it comes to income mail visiting Hours when they can use the phone ect. Privacy issue are very important in moost Prison The privacy issue will have to be faced by Most state prisons in the very near future (Note) These issue are not present in all state facility some prison have reformed these so called Issue. But a lot still needs to be Done. To improve on prisners Human right in the prison system

Parole System - Parole resembles probation in that it too provides for personal services designed to assist offenders in the Communty However, parole differ from probation in that is comes after a prison sentence has been served. Parole came to be administered by the executive branch of goverment whether in the person of the governor or in the form of a politically appointed parole board. Parole boards visit institutions, and respond to the request from prisoners and recommenendations from staff for early release. These boards have come to be much criticized for lack of clear criteria in decision making, for too much can seratism in their estimates of whether comminities will be able to accept offenders, and for failure to coordinate their desision making with prison personnel. In thinking about parole, it is use ful to hear in mind that only a comparatively small proportion of convicted offenders are even placed on parole Over 90% of misdemeanants sentenced to jail are simple released after serving their sentence. For imprisoned felons a small group To begin with, the figures are diffrant in the United States as a whole, 60 percent are released on parole, however there is great variation from state to state.

The Parol Board - when parole selection procedures were first developed, man states had a single commissoner of parole, appointd by the governor. This kind of political patronage soon led to corruption and agent deal of controvercy, and was generally abandoned after world war II Two basic models for people recommendation have replaced it.

(1)parole boards that are linked to, or actually part of, the correctional system staff and

(2)parole boards that are independent of correctional institutions and the administrators of the system A third model, a consolidation of all correctional, and parole services incorprates the most desirable aspects of the first two model In time, the indepently authorized parole-releasing authority became the most widely used model in adult corrections. As a matter of fact, today no adult parole authority is controlled directly by the staff of a personal institution The obvious purpose of this independent authority was to remove the decision making procedure from the atmosphere while an independents board may well be more objective that the correctional bureaucracy in making parole reommendations it is not a perfect system Board members lack of knowledge about the programs, policies and conditions within the prison creates an organizational gap, critics have argued, that causes, unnecessary. Conflict between prison authorities and the boards. Most parole boards operate by assigning cases to individual board members, who review the cases in detail and then make recommendations to the board as a whole. In most cases the recommendations of the individual member is accepted, but sometimes the assembled board will request more information At this point, the prisner will often be asked to appear. Some states send individual board members to the institutions to interview the inmate, and the prison staff others convene the entire board at the various institutions on a regular schedule. If inmates do not meet whatever mysterious standards the board has established for parole, their sentence are continued and they are flopped. In the case of acceptance, they are prepared for turn over to the adult board A major problem in the administration of parole decisions lies in the tendency of most boards to disreegard the right of offenders to know what standards they are expected to meet, and if they fail the reason for it. This criteria problem also affects the correctional staff, who should the rules of the game. So they can guide inmates in the direction desived by the parole board.

Conditions For Parole - The rules for conditional release develope under Irish system from the basis for most parole stipulations ever today The conditions for parole should be related to the objectives of a parole system as follow

(1) Release of each person from confineament at the most favorable time with appropriate consideration to requirments of justice, expections of subsequent behavior, and cost

(2) The largest possible number of successful parole completions

(3) The smallest possible number of new crimes committed by released offender

(4) The smallest possible number of violent acts committed by released offender

(5) An increase of general comminity confidence in parole adminstation The parole system has helped million of criminal Get a new start In live, and without this system Million of criminal would still be in prison for more years then required.

Parole based on rase, age, Gender location

Parole based on raise-Black male, white male, Black female White female

Black male - Black male on the parole system represents 6 out of 10 people natinal. Most black male on parole are located in the south. The average age of black male on parole is age 20 To 24

White male - White male on parole are young male between The av age of (19-23) Most white male on parole Are located in western state. After the ages of 24, parole by white males stable off.

Black female - Black fefmale on parole are usually young by (20-24) Most black female on parole are located in souther state. After age 25 Black female on parole stables off.

White female on Parole - White female on Parole are young women around age 20 To 24 Most white female shwo are on parole are in the lower econimic scale. The average of most white female is between the age of 20 To 24 Most white female on parole are located in the western part of the unites state. One state in particular which has The most female on parole in the state of California, which has over 25,000 white female on the parole system there. Finnal The Parole system gives criminal a second chance to do better with Ther lives, without this system criminal threwout north America would be involved longer in a already over crowed Prison system. Critics say The system needs overhauling because there is some loopholes for criminal who will find any way to get out of jail time as quick as possible. All and All parole varys from state to state and May Opinion The parole system is good system and should not have any change in the near future.

Victem of crime

If you keep one eye on your TV sets, and one ear on your Raido You will see crime victem, are mad as hell. In Amerca we pay very little attention to the needs for victems Crimes to victem such as murder, rape, assault, robbery and arson total about 11 billion each year less visble are the lost wages and the cost of pain, and suffering by victims, which comes to 191 billion victim is not uniquely American It began centuries ago in the middle ages, when the state assumed the right to restitution became converted under criminal law into a fine that went to the state. so complete was the neglect of the victem that until the mid 1960 there were neither any studies or victems nor any attempts to collect comprehensive data about them One importent aspect of the rediscovery of the vitems dates from 1965 when the president commission on crime turned its attention to how much vicimization actually occurs. It had long been recognizes that large numbers of crime went unreparoted to the police. The question was How many? The research efforts were most comprehensive. The key study sponsored by the sommission was conducted by National Opinion Research Center. a large social science orgnization specializing in public opinion surveys It used a holds surveyed slightly less than 20 percent reported that a least one person in the house hold had been criminally victimized in some way during the previous year overall the study found that about twice as much crime was reported to interviewers as was reported to police authorities. Surveys of crime victems as well as other studies, allow is to get a perspective on how the often-forgotten victem fits into the picture of crime. Several intersting Conclusion have emerged.

(1)Victems come from social groups remarkably similar to those of offenders.

56

(2)The age and sex groups most likely not to report crimes to the police are the ones most likelu to be victimized, and

(3)some violent crimes may be victim-precipitated

When asked why offences were not reported to the poliece victems gave two kinds of reasons. One, the perception that nothing could be done" was an important reason for not reporting rape, and robbery The other, the victems belief that the matter was "private" or not important enough, was cited as one of the first reasons may reflect low expectations for the police, and the criminal justice system, the other raises the Question wheather some criminal acts deemed serious under the law are actually jugded as serious by these involved in them.

<u>Victem based on race, gender, age, location</u>

Blacks Race and socieconimic status are important characteristics of crime victims. Perhape the most telling figure is that more black were murdered in the United States between 1985 To 1999 Then the entire Vietnames was. Homicide is the leading cause of death to innercity blacks One extensive analysis of the mediccal problems of the victems of violent assault shows that blacks are more likely to require over night hospitalization because of injury suffered in crime

<u>Black males</u> - Black males are victem of violent crime more than any Gender. Among youths age 14 to 17 the black males victimization rate is 65.9 per 100,000 in the population the white male rate is 8.5 percent. Black male over the age of 25 vicemization stables of to 40 percent per 100,000. Most black male who are victem of vilent crimes Is located in souther states. Fivve state in particular are Florida, Georga, North Carlina, South Carlina, Alabama.

<u>Black Female Victems -</u> Black female who are victem of crime are usually in the lower economic backet. Black Female who are now profesional women with Income of less then 10000 a year are likely to be victem of crime Then Profesinal black women . Most Black Female Victem of crime are located in large metropolitan city. The average age of most black female victem are between (18 To 24) Most black female Fictem

of crime are located in The southern metropliton City such ass Maimi FL, Atlanta George. Memphis, Tenn.

White Victem of Vilent Crime - As stated early white victem of crime are mostly male, young In located in western state. Compared To other gender. while male victemization is 10 per every 100,000 people depending on the location Most White Male who are victem of crime are young males, 18 To 22 Most Crime commited to white males are. Gang Vilence, Car Jacking, Domestic Vilence ect. Most white males who are victem of crime are single, and are in the lower ecinimic bracket. most crime commited by white male are the same age group, and same gender as them self.

White females - White female are victem of crime are usally located In large metropolitan area. Most white female who are victem of crime are young between the age of(18 and 22) Mostly located in western state one state in particular is the state of California were there is over 10 million white female in that state along Crimes against white female are, purse snathing, car jacking, and rape ect Compared To black female in the same age group. These crimes against them are 20 to eveery 10,000 people in that state.

Older Victem of Crime - Older Victem of crime (ages 65 and older) are on the raise in all 50 state. Older men and women are target of crime such as Iurressfraud, speepstakes, vaction scams, ect. Most Eldery Victem are located in the Midwestern region of the country.

Older Victem of crime based on race, and location

black older men victem of crime - black older men over the age of 65 are victem of crime More so then black female, or white female Mostly black older male who victem of crime prelocnted In large citys In the south were there Is Millions of black male in That age group. Crime against black males over the age of 65 are, Car jacking, Gang banking, and pickpocking by young people.

White Female Crime over age 65 - white elderly female over the age of 65 are victem of crime more so then black female in the same age group most Elderly white women who are Victem of rim are located in small town in the Midwest. According to many Crimolgest crimes against white Elderly women are, Vaction scams, Iurress froud, And social secity checks being stolen by Family members. These crimes against white female occur more so to them then white male black female, or blacks male In there same age group, and location.

Black Female over the age of 65 - black female over the age of 65 are crime victem less then Black male, White male, and white females, In there same age group. Most Black Female who are victem of crime are located In large City In the eastern part of the United States Crimes against black Female over the age of 65 are Braking and entering (there homes) Robbery (strong arm), and pintey theift.

white Males over the age of 65 White male over the age of 65 are Victem of crime more than black male, white female, and Black Female In there same age group. Most White male who are victem of vilent Crime are located in southern part of the united states. Crimes against white male in that age group are Investment Fraud, back fraud, and credit card Fraud. The social resemlance between offenders and victims of crime is striking according to the uniform Crime Report data for single victem-single offenders criminal homicides in 1980 To 1998 percent of whites were killed by other whites and 95 percent of blaccks by other blacks similarly, 82 percent of male victims were killed by other males but in an exception to the general pattern, only 9 percent of females were killed by other females Other more detailed examination of homicide have painted a similar picture roughly nine out of ten homicides involve people of the same race. Roughly two out of three Involved peopl of the same sex. Although data on age are affected by the way age categories are broken down. the typical murder Involves a person in there twenties Killing another only slighly older In extending analysis of offenders and victims to aggravated assault, it has been found that the proportions of offenders, and victims of the same social category are similar to those in criminal homicide Ninety percent of rapes also involve two people of the same race However there are some age differences amoug the people involved In rape on the average offender are four to five years older than their victims

Not only do victims and offenders in serious person to person violent crimes especially homicide, forcible rape, and assault have similar. social characteristics as we have already seen they are also often involved in a previous interactive relationship A further point needs to be made here the victem may have had diveit involvement, and compliaty in the sequence of actions that led to the crime.

The City -The rate of violence against house hold members in cities has been stable for two decades hitting 43.2 incidents for evvery 1,000 households in 1992. The suburban rates per 1,000 household it has declined since the 1970's The rural rates-25.2 per 1,000 what infuriates a growing number of city dwellers is the knowledge that local police do not, or cannot bother with pretty crimes like thefts from auto Such crimes classified as personal snathings and pocket pickings) take place about 12 million times each year. twice the violence total Insurrance agents often picking up the burden of dealing with these crimes. Although smaller, there are similar substantial differences for each major violent crime. Suburban areas resemble medium sized cities and rural areas show lower rates than urban areas of any size sharp rural-urban differences are also apparent in the finding on city in particular were crime rates are sky rocketing is the city of Atlanta. Just as former mayor Andrew Young was trying to win a gubernatorial bid, and the city. Atlanta representing the united state in the 1996 olympic officials. Atlanta, was recently ranked as the number one in serious crimes for the second year in a row by the FBI. In a report released reasoning the city ranked highest amoug all cities with populations of 300,000 or more according to the report Atlanta has 210 reported serious crimes per 1,000 residents Miami ranked second with 189 per thousand, and Dallas was third with 168 Atlanta's murder rate is six per 10,000 which is lower than in the District of Columbia which reported seven per 10,000. But Atlanta's murder rate is twice as high as in New York ccity where three out of ever 10,000 residents are killed. Serious crimes include murder, assault, rape, and, burglary. The crimes do not include drug offences As a result, many crime exxperts Question the accuracy of FBI. report.

Table 2 City size and crime Rates, Overall Violent Crime Murder, Forceible Rape Robbery and Aggravated and Assult.

City Size	Number of city	overall violence	murder	Forcible rape	Robbery	Aggravated assault
1,000,000	5	176.6	27.8	62.2	1108.8	527.8
500,000-999	18	1211.1	20.2	76.2	687.4	527.8
250,000 - 499,999	32	1286.4	26.9	84.5	640.6	427.2
100,000 - 249,999	112	826.4	13.1	37.9	349.6	540.3
50,000- 99,999	272	583.7	7.4	29.0	228.0	407.3
25,000 49999	594	451.9	5.7	20.1	154.8	310.4
10,000	1500	342.3	4.5	16.4	92.5	262.5
-10,000	5670	291.0	4.0	31.7	54.5	225.3
suburban areas	1104	372.2	7.3	17.7	112.0	216.0
Rural area -	2604	179.4	7.0	15.7	22.1	241.1

source FBI Federal Bureau Investigation (FBI) uniform Crime Report 1995 Government Printing office.

Things to do to avoid being a victem of crime - No safety rules can protect the law abiding from being hit by random fire from crazed gun men, but there are way to reduce the odds in other kind of attack People are picked as crime victims because they are attractive in some way. That usually mean the victim is along or has what a criminal wants Most street criminals are interesting in getting their booty, and leaving undefeated, National Crime Prevention Counsel Some basic strategies

(1) Act smart - The council recommends walking with confidence staying in well lit busy areas, walking in groups at Night being aware of your surroundings, wearing shoes and clothes that allow freedom of movement and trusting your instincts It is most often wise to give up your valuable If thats what they thug is after

Luckup - Car jacking has received a lot of attention, but a more common crime is car theft some 1.6 million were reporting in 1997 More than 200,000 vehicles are stolen each year in the united states because drivers leave key in the ignition.

Dont go - Avoid getting into an assailants car if at all possible victem rarely survive attacks after being forced into a car if you need to go some were. Try to take public transportation or a cab, or catch a ride from family and friends.

Dont open your door for stranger - Remember wheen you were a child and your mother or father told you never to open the door for stranger, well that sayings is still alive and well today Opening the door for starnger is inviting trouble into your home. If a person comes to your home saying they are working for the gascompany, telephone company water company ect Ccall the gas company. Phone company ect to verify If thy do work there Its better to be safe then sorry.

Dont exept phone Calls from strangers - Exept phone calls from stranger. If you exept phone calls from stranger ask Them want they want. Who they want to speak to And how they get the number. If you dont exept phone calls from them. They will Pinpoint were you live. And may show up at your door uninvited. These days you may not want to speak to anyone any ways.

Pick your friends wisely - Having friends in todays world is very resky. if you are over the age of 30 Your best friend should be you spouce, and family (If any) Having friends are good. for a health live. But if thereare backstabbing you or deseving you. There friendship is not worth a heal of beans.

<u>Dont talk to stranger</u> - Talking to stanger, will give them Information about you. If you do talk to stranger keep it small talk the weather, who won the game. footbal, baseball, basketball ect. Never tell them were you live, or about your family, or were you work. What they dont know wont hurt them.

<u>Avoid eye Contact</u> - looking at stanger, only invited trouble. Avoid looking at stanger as much as posible will help afoid trouble. To you down the road.

<u>Dont carry large amount of cash</u> - Carrying large amount of money invites trouble. If you travel alot it would be advisable to use your creditcard (if any) and if you own more then one credit card your Try to cary only one card at a time.

<u>Dont blame yourself</u> - The national organization for vitem Assistance tells victem not to blame themself when they dont react the way that they would have preferred. When attacked people revert to primitive behavior fueled by a rush of adrenalin. If your attackers have an assault weapon pointed at your head, its not the ideal time to duke it out with them unless you're convinced there going to kill you any way It your decision whether , or not you want to go down fighting. "be prepared-people intent on fighting back should be prepared mentally and physically. Assume that the criminal is already prepared to use force The smartest preventive mea svre against an assault is a self-defence course. Self-defense instructors point to new studies showing that women who fight back are less likely to be raped potential students should be choosy, seeking well-respected nonexorbitent programs that teach more than just physical defenses, in case the physical techniques fail Examples include being firm and repetitious in explaining what you want the assailent to do

<u>Use defensive weapons</u> - If you plan to use a defensive weapons seek training to reduce the risk that they can beturned against you. Heres a list of the most popular defensse weapons on the market today.

<u>Pepper Spray Pen</u> Conveniently disguised as a normal ink pen Easy to carry out in the open any were. Peppermint pray pen is one of the most

popular defense weapons on the market today. Mostly used in large city in the eastern part of the united state. Retail price 15.95

Key chain Pepper Spray - The slimmest spray available Marketing it the easiest, and most conveniet item to carry Contains the strongest chemials allowed by law. A single blast will completely disable attackers in less than one second even those under the Influence of drugs or alcohol) withoutcausing any permenent injuries! Also effective against vicious animals Contains untravolet dye for easy police identification Its the only spray available with the keys positioned at the top of the sprayer-test show this allows you to use the spray Quicker which is vital in case of an attack also consider this when in the can, all other sprays required you to physically turn off the engiwe and remove the key for use-with ours you simply pull down, and its ready. Mostly used by Female in there mid 20's located mostly in the midwest. In large citys Price 10.95

Personal Alarm - Emits a high-pitched ear piercing siren-like sound which can alert help in any situation! use on purses, breif cases, luggage ect. to prevent loss These alarms are also Ideal for use (to detect intruders) In your home on the doors and windows or while traveling! Mostly used in wesern state and in large city out west Price 14.95

Self Defense Items - Contains light for convenience and security to light dark paths It can also be used to temporarily blind any attacker! shoots a stun gas that completely disables even the biggest criminal with a single shot! The alarm can be sounded to alert help and scare off would be assailants All three can be used individually or simultaneously making it one of the finest compact security products you can own. Self defense Item are mostly used by women in the age group of 24- to 30 mostly white. And these items are mostly used in large metropliatan City in the south. Price 31.95

Stun Guns - All of our stun guns are unique and very effective in stopping criminals in their tracks It like having your very own guardian angle-they work on the musuclar and nevral system leaving the body unable to function for 5-10 minutes with no permananent injury They casue instant disorientation loss of balance, and muscle control - completely immobilizing a would be attacker For added safety, the current cannot pass through to your body This This defense Idea is mostly used by White Male In there 30's and 40's most white males who usse this Idem is located in the suburan in the southwest. Price 36.95 Retail

GLS MINI Stun Gun with Alarm - Not only do you have 80,000 volts of power in your hand, but this slim and compact, unit comes with the added saftey, and convenience of a personal alarm built right in to scare off the attacher and alert help GLS MINI stun gun are very popular in rural comminity In the south, mostly used by White Male age 30's and 40's and black female In the same age group retail Price 70.00

Titan ZF-Mini stun Gun - 100,000 volts of reassurance for those of you who think you can never have to much power when it comes to protecting you life. These gun are very Popular In the blak community thewout north Ameca mostly used by black male in there late 20's and mid 30's suggestive retail Price 60.00

Titan-K 200,000 volt stun Baton with alarm - what makes batons superior to others is the addition of the personal alarm Get this special zin baton and pay less than one without alarms ideal for home and auto protection This ideam is very popular to single women with children, who spend large amount of time in the home. Mostly used by White females (age 30-40) In rural community in the northwest. Price 99.50

These Ideam are very popular threwout north Ameca and canda. when it comes to protect yourself, and your family. make sure you consider these ideam to help prevent being another satistic. Finnal There is over 100 million abused Amercan from being victem of vilent crime. Victem rights movement are starting to get more Involved with victem who have been victems of vilent crime In all 50 state To contact The National organization Call 1800 Crime. Also Many state now provide for restitution to victems who have lost property Some states allow victems to be compensated for injuries or damages suffered, the compensation comming from a state fund amassed though fines Another step is to involve victem In court proceedings-In particular, in sentencing and plea bargainning decision Finnally women who are victems of rape are now interviewed by Female police officers and given greater protection from public humiliation while testifying as witnesses Each of these provision has merit but non is universal or even widespread.

What is the goverment and state roles In Control Crime

Federal state, and local govermment Is America spend nearly 39 billion annually, for protection of it citizen Threw police forces, and Federal officer. In this section we will look at the state role In Control crime, and what (If any) change should be made to Improve there role in the crime picture. Also we will look at the federal goverments role In crime and what change (If any) should be made To Improve There position in the future First of states

States - No reasonable person would Question the right of the state to protect its citizens It certainly has the right to restrains people who are incapable of controlling their action. A person convicted of a crime Should like fims, and loss of privileges, Restitution states Through criminal Laws, and the criminal Justice system seeks To

protecte society and its citizens.

rehabilitate persons who have committed crimes.

To punish persons who have committed crimes.

Sentence persons who have committed crimes.

Seriousness of the crime.

harm to the victim or society.

Need to deter others.

Need to protect society.

Need to maintain supervision over the offender.

possiblty of rehabilitation

not all state following these guidelines These varition from state to state.

In enacting criminal laws through the use of the police power, the state is regulating the conduct of citizens within the state by telling them what they may not do or what they must do The state may not regulate conduct arbitrarily In enacting criminal law, the state must be able to show That there is a compelling public Needs to regulate the conduct the state seeks to regulate and that the power to regulate is within the police power o the state The US supreme Court held in (lawtony steal) that it must appear first that the intrests of the public generally require such interference, and that the means are not unduly oppressive upon individuals That the law does not contiavence the US Constitution or infringe on any of the rights granted, or secured by the US Constitution or the constitution of the state. That the language of the statute, or ordinance clearly tels people what they are not to do (or what they must do) and that the law prohibits only the conduct that may be forbiden Most criminal law is found in he statutes of each state, and in the statutus of the federal goverment Criminal law can also be found in commercial sanitation, health, financial, and tax administrative regulations that have criminal sanctions These regulations are enacted by state, and Federal administrative, and regulatory agencies A few sections of state contitutions, and one section of the US constitution criminal law criminal law on rare occasions can be found in the common law of some states

Most Amercan state have used common law crimes in their early histories some of these crimes were taken from English common law crimes others were defined by judges in those sates Today in the United states almost half the states have abolished common law crimes within their jurisdictions In the state that have not abolished common laws crimes it is unusual for a person to be charged with a common law crimes ecause all states legislative bodies have enactedhundreds of statutory criminal offenses a prosecutor who is charging a statutory offence is on the much safer ground than he, or she would be in charging a common law crimes which immediately leaves the charge vulnerable to attack. Since most crimes are crimes only against a state, only the state may prosecute for that crimes Cities counties towns, villages, and other manicipalities are created by state to assist in providing necessary governmental services. Because municipolities own their existence to the state they are not separate sovereigns and are only an arm of the state In recognizing that the only sovereign in a state is the state government. States grant to municipalities the right to enact penal-type ordinan ecstriable in municipal courts a person who is tried again for the same offense in a state court (violation of state law) The prosecution for the municipal, or dinance violations places a defendant in jeopardy, and bars another prosecution under state statutes for the same offense.

Punishment has always been part of all criminal offenses, The concepts of crime, and punishment are insparable criminal codes are called penal codes, or penal laws in some states including that violations of such laws are subject to punishment Crimes are classified in terms of their punishment For example, Section 1.04 of the Model Penal Code states that an offense for which a sentence of imprisonment is authorized constitutes a crime Section 1.04 (2) of the model Penal Code states that a crime is a felony if the punishment is imprisonment in excuses of one year Many states, in seeking to provide for more uniform punishments used a classification system for penalties There may be five classes of felonies (class A through class E) with each class having a statutory punishment. Misdemeanors are usually classified from class A through class C.

Many cities and states have created career criminal progress such programs ordinarily operate under statutes providing additional and longer sentences for repeat offenders.

established special career-criminal unites in the offices of police and prosecutors that vigorously investigate frequently committed crimes auto that, (example) speed up prosecuton if it is determimed that the person is a career criminal, or repeater. definition of these offenses can be found in the state statute. One city in particular which is doing there best to stop the spread of crime is the city of Houston, Houston which report a 22 percent crime drop in the 4 years sence it established a major police overtime program adding the equivilant o several hundred officer to a 4,500 member force. The bill also will probably fund boot camps for nonviolent offenders prison for violent juveniles school security, anti gang enforcement, and drug courts. that funnel low-level drug offenders to treatment rather than to jail more debatable are various provisions of the ill. Also the city of Houston has set up program to help victem of crime. Justice for all is a program which has helped thousand of victem of vilent crime get Repraisals for there pain, and suffering from there acused.

Three strike policy - Some state are using raticle measure to stop the spread of crime in major citys in there state. New bill which are being Introduced by state Legestaters In Texas which will give criminal stifer sentence for certain crimes which will make it tougher on criminal to get parol, and longer mandatory sentence. Texas inmate serve only 11 percent of their sentences as compared with prisoners in California, who serve 50 percent of their allotted time. That figure will go down for California this year because the state also passed three strike law and, like Texas is unwilling to come up with the money for enough new jails to house the additional prisoners, Th nonpartism office of Legislative Service In New Jersey analyzed the impact of three strikes laws, and concluded that for every inmate who is not paroled as a result of this bill an additional 80,000 in constructive costs, and 1 million in operating costs would be incurred over the life time of that inmate The three strike policy is counterproductive Most crimes are committed by young people In deedafter a century of experimenting with ways to rehabilitate criminals, from isolation cells to tottal lock down. The three strike policy has its good points and bad But all, and all most people who live in those state favor this retical approach to crime.

Chain gangs - Back in the 1920's most prison would lock Down Prisoners by chain them together to lessing there escape. In one state this retical approach is back. The state of Alabama is using this old idea to set prsadented threw out the country States legester In all 50 state are looking closley at the States of Texas and Alabamia to see If there ideas are detering crime In there state. Finnal, with 1 million people In state prison and 45,000 In county Jail. State legslatrs are focusing on the future. With the growing population of young people, and resource for them scares. Many state have decide to fight crime by building more prison. A number of state legester feel this is the best way to fight crime well Into the next centery. by locking up as many criminal as possible. Instead of reforming them to be more prouctive members of society. Many critics feel the united state is turning back the clock. To a time when we treated human beings like cattle. Instead of people with minds and idea which may find a cure for aids, or cancer.

<u>Govement role In the crime problem</u> - The American constitutional system is based on a division of powers between the national government and the states under our federal system. The National goverment are enumerated in the body of the constitution whereas those powers not delegated to the National goverment are reserved to the states, or to the people The tenth amendment anounces this principal of federalism, The federal Govement of the united state was based on Fair treatment to all of its people with the, beleve that all men are created equal, and should be able to govern themself. The federal government, unlike the states exercises no general police powers to regulate it citzenry There is no federal criminal common law Federal crime are of statutory origin They have not been passed down to us from the Magna carta as interpicted by experience and reason Although our fore fathers could have provided in the constitution that the congress had a general police power exclusive, superior or coextensive with that of the states, they did not do so. Instead they limited the powers of congress and retained to the states and people powers not otherwise confered on the federal goverment. Such restrictive grant of power to the federal goverment was the result of philosophical and political concien of the drafters against a strong centralized government within the limited areas of federal jurisdiction. there are three primary base of jurisdiction They basically evolve from the nature and character of our federal system of government dual form of government with a national centralized government and its component states Each of these primary base is related to the nature and character of that government. Parotection of Federal Interest The centralized national government has an inherent interest in protecting itself, its operations, and interests Implicit in this basis is the governments right to protect its officials, personnel, agencies property, or interests Thus, the federal government may make criminal an assault upon or injury to the President, members of congress, Judges US Attoroneys and their assistants, and other federal agents It my make criminal the counterfeiting, or forging

of its currency obligations, and securities theft of its property theft from its mails, fraud against the government or its agencies, and fraud against its revenues The government can also uphold the integrity of its function, and operations by prohibiting bribery of its officials, conflicts of interest, obstruction and interference, with its judical experations prejury in its courts, or before a grand jury similarly the goverment can prevent its services from being preverted it illicit ends, ie the use of the mails to defraud the use of mail is to extoit the use of the mail to promote, establish or carry on an illegal enterprise involviing gambling, prostitution, or narcotics not only are the governments direct interests safe guarded, but the governments in direct interest in federally Insured banks, and savings and loan associations are protected. These Include preventing the making of false statements to federal agencies, or statements designed to defraud, or mislead federal agencies. The govenments interests include the preservation of its navigable waters and the air in our environment. The federal governments interest in protecting its property has given rise to the drep of assimilative crimes the incorporation of state criminal laws in such are as as federal Indian, and military reservations, federal enclaves, and federal building.

Corpusdelicti - The government must show proximate cause or causation in all criminal cases, since it is an essential element of any crime charged Causation is related in some respects to the requirement of (corpusdelicti) proof that a crime was committed However, the two requirements are separated and distinct Corpus delicti means the body, or substance of the crime which is very important in all federal cases. Corpus delicti cannot be presumed, and must be established by legal evidence Mere hearsay, or the showing that the accused had a motive to commit a crime is not sufficient to prove corpus delicit As a general rule, curpus delicti must be established beyond a reasonable doubt It may be established not only by direct and positive evidence, but also by circumstantial evidence the general rule is that the evidence must be so sonclusive as to eliminate all reasonable doubt in showing that a crime was actually committed. If there is no evidence of the corpus delicti Most accused, May be set free according to federal Law corpus Delicti is used to prove guilt in 85% of federal cases. Including federal Homicede cases, federal wirer taping, theft of federal bank robbery, blackmail, extortion ect. The impertance of curpus delicti in this section is, Many federal cases has been resolved do to ruling conserning corpus delicts , . Most state have adopted ruling consening corpus delicti into there states Laws Corpus Delicti has changed many court desition involving federal cases corpus delict has been around for over 100 years. And will be around for another 100 years. In the federal Judical system.

Uniform Crime Report - The federal goverment has used a number of method over the years to keep up with the crime threw out north Amercia. The most frequently used publication concerning crime is the uniform crime report (UCR) published annally by the Federal Bureau of Investingation since the 1930's Although in Federal concern with crime did not begin untill the late 1870's when the Department of justice was created One section of the law establishing the department stated that it was the duty of the Attorney General to make an annual report to Congress the statistics of crime under the laws of the United states, and, far as practicable, under the laws of the several states However, this section fell into disuse almost immediately, not untill 1929 after much lobbying by the international Association of chiefs of police, and other interested groups, was there an effort to establish uniform crime reporting that attempted to standardize record-keeping practices, and provide an over all perspective on the amount of crime in the unite states. The Uniform Crime Reports Quickly became a key source of crime statistics They provide official statements about the amount of crime in the united states by reporting figures on the number of crimes reported to the state, and local police agencies. They also reported the proportion of crimes knowns that are cleared by arrest The number of arrests, and the social characteristics of persons who are arrested However, limitations of the UCR have resulted in the devvelopment of many other crime statistics programs. Problems in methodology have led to attempts to assess over all crime rate by using approaches other than uniform crime reporting-In particular, by using vitimization and self-report surveys at the same time, criminal justice agencies many of which emerged in the decades following the 1930's have found the need for detail that are more specific, and more appropriate to their concerns The results is a prollferations of crime statistics programs. An overveiw of those operating at the federal level. Dispite the number of crime statistics programs, many of the historical problems remain For one standardization of reporting is elcsive since most of the programs rely upon voluntory use by state, and local agencies of recommended uniform crime reporting procedures For another, there is still fragmentistion in the over all statistic on crime victimization studies show only indirectly the amount of crime that has come to police attention agency statistics reflect only one component of the criminal Justice system Criminal Justice statistics, and statisties from specialized, and limited programs relate to efforts of federal agencies, whereas the majority of those convicted of felonies have violated state laws. Finally there is no central agency designed to coordinate data-gathering efforts, and to provide a complete overveiw of crimes in the united states.

<u>Limitation of the Uniform Crime Report</u> - Although the Uniform Reports are our most extensive source data about crime in the United states they have been subject of much criticism, and debate, controversey has centered on three major areas (1) the particular offenses which should be included the gaps between reported crime, and arrests and statistical errors related to the techniques, and scope of the data-gathering efforts since UCR data are so widly used.

<u>Uniform crime offenses</u> - The most important criticism of (UCR) concerns the offenses that are, or should be included in the reports. For the most part, the Uniform Crime Reports measure person-to person offenses. Although the category all other offenses make it appear that the figures are complete, the crimes which fall into the scope of (UCR) are typically those committed by the poor the young, and the relatively powerless. Certain serious crime such as kidnapping, and sky jacking are not listed. Serarately by type some significant corporate crimes such as violation of antitrust laws, enviromental pollution, and marketing of unsafe products, are not listed. because they are enforced by other federal agencies. Neither do most crimes against organizations find their way into the reports. Because they are usually handled by private rather than public police agencies, still other crimes, such as income

tax evasion, are left out altogether nor is there a separate category for organized crime, although arrests of organized crime figures may appear under gambling drug abuse, or prostitution, and commercialized vice, while serious crime such as fraud offenses, category larceny-theft with the result that many comparatively minor theft crimes can be classified instance, one may Questions whether theft of bicycles, and motor vehicle accessories, which together account for 30 percent of all larcenies, should be considered as a problem comparable to murder, assault, rape, or robbery

(2)Gaps The second criticism of the uniform crime Reports concerns the gap between crimes that really occur, and those that are reported. And the gap between crimes that are reported and arrests. There is, to begin with, an immense amount of unreported, and uncounted crime It occurs but it is not reported, or, if reported to the police, it is not recorded for (UCR) purposes. Unreported crime can range from trival thefts to murders which may be discovered only by change. In order to obtain estimates of the amount of crime that really occurs. Criminologists have developed victim surveys which will be discussed below. Generally, victem surveys have found that reported crime is only one-half, or one-third of the amount mentioned to survey interviews. In addition to to gap between real and reported crime, there is another between reported crime and arrests. In a given year police make well over 15 million arrests. a rate of 5705 per 100,000 people. However, the large number of arrests can be misleading Since arrest-statistics measure the number of arrests the number of individuals involved may be considerably less than the 15 million. noted, because some persons may be arrested more than once during a given year. More over, nearly one out of every four arrests is for alcohol-related offenses especially driving under the Influence and "drunkenness" Only about one in five arrests(30 percent to be exact) Index offense. The gap between reported crime, and arrests is evident in the low percentage of crimes cleared by arrest for the serious offenses, the over all arrest clearance rate is about one in six. The clearance rate varies for the specific offenses that make up the crime index from a high of 72 percent for murder to a low of 14 percent, for motor vehicle theif. The proportion of all reported part

1 crime cleared by all arrest has interestingly enough, remained near 20 percent for each of the past 20 year despite enormous Increased in the number of reported crimes. The fact that only a small proportion of crimes are cleared by arrest means that the characteristics of arrested persons may not be indicative of all persons who are actually committing crimes. Those who are arrested tend to be male, young black and poor. who commits four out of five offenses which are not cleared by arrest?

Statistical Problems - The third criticism concern (UCR) data has to do with methods of data gathering which can play an important part in the compilation of crime statistics Perhaps the most basic problem is that statistics are gathered by the more than 15,000 local law enforcement agencies. which voluntary cooperate in the uniform crime reporting. system administered by the Federal Bureau of Investigation. This approach is made necessary, because police departments are organized locally rather than federally, or by state In the early years of uniform crime reporting fewer local agencies chose to cooperate in the system, so that (UCR) statistics covered only half of the united states population (rural areas). However, over the years the number of participating agencies has increased, so that the reports now cover about 98% of the total population. Gathering the UCR statistics locally means that they are subject to errors differenses in interpretation of incidents, or arrests, and manipulation on the part of officials. In the past years officially reported crimes in various localities have shown some sharp charges from one year to another. The FBI now exerts greater diligence in the efforts to standardize crime reporting In particular, it checks for error when it receives crime reporting In particular, it checks for error when it receives reports indicating any significant increase or decrease over the previous reporting period It also compares agency reports against the experience of similar agencies, and conducts seminars, and workshops in crime reporting Increased Increased technical sophistication in counting has influenced the number of crimes reported Centralized reporting, often with the use of special telephone numbers, has taken reporting out of the hands of local precinct commanders and given police cheifs centralized control over it Many departments have computerized their reporting processes. The necessity of reporting come crimes to insurance companies and the undespread publicity about crimes also encourage people to report victimizations All these changes promise a more efficient official crime reporting system. At the same time, they may also means that the apparently higher reported crimes rate of recent years may in part be the result of reporting factors rather than an increase in crime itself is computed can be immensely misleading Simple adding the number of incidents, or rates of different type of crimes together in effect makes the major offenses equal. However, can we really give homicide, and larceny-theft equal ranking? Note also that 90 percent of reported offenses are property crimes burglary, larceny, and motor vehicle theft Only 10 percent are violent crimes: homicide, rape assault, and robbery. In other words although we often think of violent crimes when we hear the term crime rate" The crime rate is basically composed of property crimes change in Violent crime-for example, a doubleing of the homicide rate-would have virtually not impact on the total crime index, relatively small changes in it rate may have been considerable impact on the total rate Even with their limitation, the (UCR) data are still the most extensive source of information on crime, and on police activited, especially arrest; and the trend is toward more reporting, and more uniformity in methods of reporting at the same time, it must be said that whether the Uniform Crime Report are useful souce of date for criminology, and criminological research is an open Question while some have argued that they may be Quite useful if modest demands are made of them for instance, they can provide clear indications of which cities have more crimes than other. The limitation of (UCR) statistics, and debates about them have stimulated a great deal of research designed to develope other ways to estimate the amount of crime in the united states Victem survey, self-reported criminal behavior, a third is the attempt to generate dollor estimates of crimes, Since these other approaches have produced estimates of crime rates that differ markedly from these of the Uniform Crime Reports, it is important to have a clear understanding of all of the them. So you will be able to have a clear cut veiw of different approach used to keep track of the crime problem In The united states.

Law enforcement Assistance Act 1965 - The turbulance of the early 1960's prompted federal enactment of the Law Enforcement Assistance Act of 1965 That act, designed to test the valuse of granting federal funds to assist local law enforcement, was a symbol of things to come after release of the finding of The Johnson Adminastration criminal Justice commission entitled The CHallenge of Crime in a Free Society (1967) legislation was introduced to vastly expand the Law Enforcement Assistance Act, with direct grants to state, and local governments focusing on causation research prevention, and control of crime. But the US Senate moves slowly the bill was dead locked in committed when Congress was shocked from its apathy by the assassination of presidential aspirant Senator Robort Kenndy. This dramatic demonstration of the Nations needs for more effective crime control prompted Quick passage. The final version of the bill, known as the omwibus Crime Control and Safe Street Act of 1968, replaced direct grants to local governments with block grants to the state, but was otherwise passed substantially as submitted This far-researching Act implemented by the Law Enforcement Assistance Administration (LEAA) provide billions of dollars to states for action programs research education evaluation, training and administration of the criminal justice system Amendments in the 1970 created category of funds especially earmarked for corrections As part of LEAA the Law Enforcement Educations Program has funneled more than 260 million to at least 300,000 or imunal justice student since 1968. The policy change embodies in this act was a reacted a new awarness of the realities of local political structures Not since 1929, when President Hoover established the National Commission on Law Observance and Enforcement commonly know as the Wickersham Commission. Had the executive office undertaken an in-depth examination of crime In America The Great Depression World War II The korean war, and subsequent adjustments to peace all led a searies of presidents to assign a low priority to criminal justice reforms. vehicles guns electronic, and office equipment, and couterfeit and stolen credit cards

Internal Revenue Stings - In addition to againt computer network undercover agents, use of Informents the IRS is using broad and sophisticated sting operations In such operations, false documentation and laundered government money is used to infiltrate, and penetrate businesses suspected of tax fraud.

SL scandals of the 1980s During the 1980 one of the most costly, and least talked about scandals in the United state was the SL scandals. Goverment banks across the country were riped of for over 500 billion dollor. The cost to the united state Tax payers. for these crime, will take them nearly 100 hundreds to recover for this crime of the centrey.

Strike operation To Political figures - Once in a while a stike operation will pin point political figure In a high profile postion. One of the most famaus stink operation In reason years. was conducted by the FBI in washiigton DC major Marowbarry was caught using the illegal drug (crack cocain) and was indited on 12 count for misuse of his office. and was releved of his duty. But was voting back in office In 1994 and took office in Januarary of 1995. finnal Sting and scam operation will be used by goverment more In the future with technolgy better then it was 10 years ago. You will see the goverment utilizing there vase resource to curtain the growth of crime In ever aspect of owr lives

The out break of violence on the streets of America in the early 1960s changed all that Form the embattled ghettos of Los Angeles and Detroit to the assassination of the president in Dallas events highlighted the problems of crime, and violence across the Nation on July 23, 1965 President Lyndon B Johnson established a commission on Law Enforcement, and Administration of justice with a mandate to examine every area of the American criminal justice system. The commission report, The challenge of crime in a Free Society, and its more detailed papers have become the basic reference points for progress on all fronts of the criminal justice system.

sting operation by the govement - In recent years law enforcement agencies have used deception to obtain evedence against persons committed crimes Sting, and scamoperation have received the most public attention and have been the most successful The LEAA Law Enforcement) Assistance administration) reported that it had funded nearly 70 sting operation across the country. As a result thousand of arrest warrants were Issued. Such sting operation have helped solve crimes such as murder, assult, rape, burglary rings, and organized crime. example of some of these sting used in the past few years are as followed.

Operation Hornets Nets - Law enforcement officers in the Los Angeles area recovered 23.5 million in stolen goods and made 460 felony arrests in what is called the biggest sting operation conducted by that time The sting operation was funded with a 100,000 investment from the US justice department, and operated almost a year in 1983 until the task force ran out of money. Property recovered include

Contract with America - In todays world the political power is changing repetly In Washington, new face new ideas. To the same old problems of crime In Amerca. With the new Republean majority In congress, and new speaker of the house. The Republican majority feels crim can be altered with ratical change. The republican majority Is approaching crime In America very conservetily High on the republican list in the fight against crime is the following.

(1)More money to fund state prison in all 50 statements(2)lesser reform of prisoner

Acording to most republican the way to foot the cost of more prison would be

(1)Cut Affariimative action program very unpopular To black (In low Income) bracket

(2)Higher taxes - very unpopular to all Americans.

(3)Cut Medicare - very unpopular to senior citizen over the age of 65. these medical ideas are very unpopular To millions of Americans. But In my feiw ratical change must be made when it come to the crime problem. Even If it efects where half of the American population econimical and politicaly.

The Clinton Crime bill - During the Clinton administration he had his own veiw on fighting crime. For his part clinton forces promise to mumT a balance attack on vilence. The expresident thinks the debate between prevention and punishment is a false one The Clinton Crime bill has the following points

(1) Ban on deadly assault weapons.

(2) Expand the Death peanlity.

(3) 100,000 more police office on the stree mostly in large citys.

(4) More Money on Prison.

(5) less money on drug treatment programs.

The most likely clinton action against crime in the short term-expanding police forces, and prisons tend to becestly and yet might only reduce crime marginally For example the prison-building boom of the 1980s had little effect on violent-crime rates. The clinton crime bill has its pros, and cons, all and all the plain has its supporter and nonsapporter In washington. A Clinton antiviolence team is examining some basic elements of the problem, of crime in America society. Including family strife, hate crimes, and the role of the media. It could lead to the creation of an unofficial Department of violence. to coordinate disjointed federal aid programs Clintons agency violence working group has send him a plan to short-circuit violence, particularly amoung the young people in society. The panel has identified effective local programs, and wants to create a clearing Quickly about solutions that have, worked elsewhere. The Clinton group will urge more federal backing for providing mentors to troubles youth, and parenting, help to mothers It also will call for putting more pressure on the entertainment media to deglamorize violence major television net works already have blcs of time to examining the violence problems in owr society. Federal housing officials soon will initiate Project Crackdown to claim down on crime in public housing one particular housing project the goverment has pinpointed is Chicago mass housing project, were the goverment has decide to take over. Projects there do to the large amount of drugs, and gangs which are located there. Including expansion of the Federal witness protection program to teanants who live in those areas who observe crime. The group will push for more emphasis on school safety, included expantion of a safehaven program to keep schools open into the evening. This measure are very important to Million of people and communty across Amercia. And with resources scarce at all level of government, the best hope for progress against violence is at the local level where grass reot organiztions from East to West must find ways to solve there own commutys. After all they are the ones who have to live In them. Finnal, libral consertive, moderate In washington. All have there own ideas on how to approach the new wave of crime In Amercan Some ideas were heard before some we heaved the Crime approach by are politician in washington will make a profound effect on all of us. And will defently be a issue in future ellection, in all 50 state in this country In The US.

The Gun Control Debate

For years gun control Has been a issue Threwout the united state. Everone has there own opinion about Gun control. There has been survey In all regions of the country. From people from all walks of live about the gun Issue Many people feel Gun are the single most Important Issue facing are society today. In this section we will look at the beginning of the gun control Issue the Pros, and Cons of gun in todays world were the guns are mostly located. The Goverment, and state role in the gun control Issue. Men and women Gun owners Monorty and Gun some solution to the Gun problem, and Gun control Issue in the future.

The beginning of the Gun Issue - The Gun Issue has been around since The country began back in the late 1700s when the second Amemdment to the US constitution was ratified in 1791 as part of the bill of rights, the newly formed united states was a frontier nation with about 4 million, or so people Firearms were essential for survival since most of the families depended on wild game as part of their subsistence Guns were also needed for self-defense because organized law enforcement agencies were not within immediate call of most population so guns were assential for protection do to the unknow and wilderness of the new frontier.

Guns today - The number of gun In America Increased from 54 million gun in 1950 to 201 million gun in 1990s. Gun are In high demand by the majorty of people In the United state while American own weapons for a number of reasons, one of the ironies in the picture of crime is that the house gun kept for self-defense is six time more likely to be used to kill someone by accident or in a Quarrel than to defend against an intruder It is also estimated that 100,000 Firearms are stolen each year primarily during house hold burglaries. Despite these problems the United States is very permissive about gun ownership and even regard it as a constitutional right.

survey taken in 1998 of a 100,000 house hold threwout the united states. Do you favor Gun Control

Ban all guns 39%

stringent control 17%

no gun control 37%

some control 43%

71% percent of those responding owned guns, and only 27 percent had been the victims of a crime involving a gun.

The hand Guns - Although there is not necessary connection between possession of a firearm and its utilization for a violent crime, the gun especially the hand gun, is a most effective weapons for criminal homicide, and robbery. It is easily concealable, and allows the offender to harm the victem. without engaging in direct personal contact as it turns out, the hand gun is the most popular weapons for criminal homicide half of reported homicides are committed with some type of firearm. And four out of ten robberies are committed with firearms. many of which are hand guns.

The handgun has become not only the number one tool of serious crime in the united states, but a common instrument in suicide. Although some countries have higher overall suicide rate than does the united states our firearm suicide by firearms in the united states than in all the other countries combined. It also follows that because of the presence of large numbers of firearms. The united state has the highest number of accidental shooting worldwide.

Except for Homicide, Most violent crimes do not Involve the use of weapons

(weapons use)	Homicide	Rape	Robbery	Assault
Firearm-	62	7	18	9
knife-	19	15	21	9
other-	13	1	9	14
unknown-	0	2	2	1
Total-	100	100	100	100

Because some victimization involve more than one type of weapon, detail may add to more than 100%

National crime Survey 1998

Estimate is based on 10 or fewer sample Estimate are not 100% reliable.

Half of all homicides are committed with hand guns

Hnad Guns	Rilfe	Shotgun	Cuting or stabing	other weapons such as clubbs poisons	Hand or feet
50%	5%	8%	19%	13%	6%

<u>Were The Gun are mostly Located</u>

Gun are located In all 50 states and owned by a varity of people. Most Gun owner are located in large metropolition City. The Guns most people own In those city are hand guns.

Eastern city states 38 million gun - 37 Million hand guns

Western city and states 49 million gun - 47 Million hand guns

Norther city and states 50 million gun - 48 Million hand guns

Souther states and citys 63 million gun - 60 million hand guns

Territory with most gun and weapons - Texas 17 million guns

Bureau of Alohol Tobacco and Firearms 1998 Data

No one knows the exact amount of guns in those location This is a rough extemt from data from bureau of alcohol Tobacco and Firearms.

Age, race, gender of most Gun owners

Age of most Gun owners-

Most gun owner age is between 18-44 Between this age group, there is beleved to be 175 million Guns owned by People in the age group. Most Guns owned by this age group of people is the hand gun. After age 44 Gun ownerhip levels off.

Gender of most Gun owners - Most Gun owners are white males between the age of 24 and 44 Most of these male are located in The southeastern part of the united states. The ownership of Gun by white males is beleved to be 130 million Gun in that age group. Most Gun owned by white Male is the hand gun.

Female Gun owners -

Gun owned by female are on the raise over the past 20 years. Most Female Gun owner are between the age of 24 To 44 Most Female Gun owner are white Most white female Gun owner are located In eastern part of the united state. The Gun owned by white females mostly is the hand gun Estimate amount 36 million

Black male Gun owners -

Black male Gun owners are uslly young between the age of 19-44 Most of these black gun owners are located in southern state. The gun mostly prefered by black males is the hand Gun Estimate amount 70 million

Black Female -

Black female who own gun are located mostly In midwestern state. The average age of most black female are between 20-26 The Gun most black female own is the hand gun Estimate amount 35 million.

Goverment and State role In the Gun Control Issue

State roles in the Gun control Issue

Gun Control is a mater leave up to the states. All states have criminal statutes. regulating the sale possesion, and use of weapons. and probably

Hs make it a criminal offense to carry a concealed weapons. In one state its Legal to carrry a firearm, and that state is Arizon. All other state and menipalities share diffrent veiws on guns mostly hand guns. With thousand of diffrent laws on the books in each state. Gun control Issue are very complicated. California attempted to pass the tougest hand gun control laws in the United states in proposition 15, Despite public opinion polls indicating that the hand gun control law would pass Proposition is lost by a vote of 60 percent to 40 perecnt

The Goverment Role in the Gun control Issue

The federal goverment has used a vairty of methods to regulate and control the spread of gun threwout the country One of the earliest federal regulation of firearms is the 1934 National Firearms act. Public Law (73-474) which forbids the interstate shipment of special weapons used for illegal use It forbids the interstate shipment without a license of sawed off shot guns, machine guns, and mufflers, and silencers for guns The 1938 Federal Firearms Act requires that Firearms manufactures, dealers importers, and other persons engaged in firearms shipments across state lines be licensed by the federal government that act also forbids the interstate hipment of all firearms to or by convicted felons, person under under indictmentm and fugitive from Justice. The Gun Control Act of 1968 public Law 90-618 bans the interstate and mmail order shipments of firearms to individuals, and provides for the licensing of dealers, manufacturers, and importers, It requires the registration of destructive devices cannons, antitank guns bazookas It bars the importation of cheap concealable foreign hand guns, such as the six dollor saturday night special, These three pieces of federal legislation do not make it difficult to obtain firearms in the unites states Guns are plentiful and easy to obtain by almost anyone persistent enough in attempting to purchase a weapons However Section 1202 of the 1968 Federal omnibus crime control act Tikle VII forbids the following person from possessing any firearms.

Clinton crime bill - one of the most Important Element in The Clinton crime bill. Is a baw a deadly assault weapons. The ban would cover all 50 state any person with the weapon. would face years, In a federal prison Another branch of goverment (the supreme court) Decide 4 To 5 To ban hand gun within a 100 feet from grade school In 1995 other laws past by goverment, would make murder with guns a federal crime punishable by death, But there no clear cut evedence that such effedence in recent years to get federal authorities into basic street level Law enforcement have had much impact.

The brandy bill - back in 1981 President eagan, and one of his cabnet members Jim brandy was shot with a cheap hand gun by John Hinkley Juner. This act along, has changed Million of people feiws about Gun control. A bill was passed In both house of congress and Then preapdent reagan which will make it tougher for people to get hand guns, and a longer time (10 days or more) before Gun dealers can okay the sale of a hand Gun. to any person. Also background checks must be done before the sale is completed. The brandy bill is enforced In all 50 state and has had a profounded effeted on Gun sale threwout the country These laws by federal goverment has spred thousand of lives threwout the united state. Lives which may have been taken by hand guns And the people who use these guns to spread death.

Some Souttion to the Gun Control Issue

Peeple from all walks of live have given ther opoion about Gun Control. Some are Good some are bad. Here my personal solution to the gun control Issue facing us today.

(1) update the second amendment.

(2) make them child prove.

(3) Make them personalised.

(4) usse tecknology to make them safer.

(5) cooling off period should be lenting.

(7) no Gun in mentally ill people hands.

(8) A National Hand Gun Hot Line

(9) Ban on the black talon bullet.

(10) Ban hand gun all together.

(11)no Gun in the hand of person under the age of 21

Update the second Amendement - Unless the second Amendment were to be changed by constitutional amendment, the power of the states to prohibit the private ownership, and possession of hand guns rests on the interpretation of the second Amendment by the US Supreme Court. There are currently two interpretation of the Second Amendment, the individualist view, and the national veiw The individualist view interprets the Second Amendment broadly and is urged by those who oppose laws forbidding the possession of hand guns, or registration requirements They argue that the Second Amendment, adn that the amendment ensure the right of individuals to bear arms to protect themselves not only from dangerous intruders against their homes, and property. but also against possible oppression by goverment itself. They point out that when the second Amendment was ratified, Americans had just created a strong central government, and that the citizens of those days feared a repetition of many abuses that strong centialized government had Imposed The National view inteerprets the Second Amendment strictly and holds that this amendment was meant to provide for strong militians of private citizens. Persons who advocate the national view argue that as the need for the mlitia No longer exists the right of individuals to keep and bear arms need longer exists because private weapons. are not longer needed either for the national defense or for emergencies many believe with updating the amendemt To deal with today person Crimes commited by guns will decrease

Make them child prove - 15 children each day are killed by hand guns In owr contry Gun manufactors must find a way to make there gun child prove. The NRA has been preaching about this for years. Statistics show that the accidents occur mostly among children of the peeple who most often misuse guns. Critics say, it up to the parent to keep guns out of children hand. Not the NRA, or gun manufactors. This Issue will be debate for many years.

Make Them personalized - With 200 million gun on the streets Gun manufators should manufactor there guns with personaly IDs or, print such as person last name, street adress, ect - This will help if gun are stolen from home (20 million each year) lost, or misplaced.

Use Tecknology to make them safer - If The United state can seen a man to the moon (40 years ago) They should be able to make gun much safer. By using safty locks, and combination locks only the owner knew how to use. There simple tecknicks can safe live be on your wildest dreams. Something gun manufators should look closly into.

Cooling off periods should be lentinged - from the period of time it take a person to get a gun in the heat of rage, from argument, from dispute, from theft whatever the reason. People need more time before they pull the treger. Cooling off peiod In most states are only a few days. Before gun dealer can sell a weapon to angry person Cooling off period I give a person time to think before they pull the trigger.

No gun in a person hand who Is mentally Ill

According to many surveys 1 third of all of us Is suffering from some sort of mental Illness. Mental Diease Can effect your thinking and judgment. Puting a gun in a person hand who has a metall diesase in all 50 state is retical but practice.

A National Heard Gun Hot Line - There are bills being Introudced In most states which will shave hand gun hot line information with local law enforcement agency to access to state records on hand gun purchases. The hot line conducts criminal background checks on those who buy handguns from licensed firearms dealers. These dealers share Information with local Law enforcement agencies, and authorities in other states a National Gun hot line has it pros, and cons. critics claim The bill exculed federal athority access to state records on hand gun purchases If the states and Federal Goverment can work together on a comprimize. The hand gun hot line bill may be successful.

Ban on the black Talon bullet - The black talon bullets is one of the most deadlest bullet manufactered to day. this bullet Kills with deadly force. In 1997 the National leading ammunition manufacturer winchester, was determined to win a shoot out with competitor Federal Cartridge, the nations No 3 bullet maker winchester was three years behind Federal in marketing a highly profitable premium line of hand gun cartridges so it ensconced its new black Talon cartridge in a black box with the words deep penetrator in red bought multipage advertisements for black Talon in gun magazines, and set up store displays of spent bullets with their characteristics six bladed-star shape The blitz worked But the new bullets also caught the eye of criminals, and then emergency room doctors. distrought over the black Talons bleeding victems. A bill that would levy a 10,000 percent tax on winchester hollow tipped black Talon bullets which are specifically designed to rip flesh. The tax would be raise the price on black Talons from 20$ to 2000$ a piece The bill was introduced by seanter patrick mognihan of New York soon after the bill was introduced, winchester, burned by bad publicity banned the cartridge from stores limiting their sale to law enforcement agencies. The ammunition industry, which has been selling nearly a half-billion dollars worth of cartridges, and shells a years is under scruting. And though manufactures have become increasingly tight business some 6,000 workers each year produce 3.9 billion rounds of ammunition, about a third of it for hand guns. Private citizens buuy seven times as much as state and local Police forces and sales are growing at up to 12% percent annually. So when criminal need to reload, the supply is plentiful The bureau of alcohol, Tobacco and Firearms notes that unlike guns which can fetch four and five times their retail value in illegal street sale ammunition carries no black-market markup, although some stores sold their last black Talons for up to three times the regular price Federal laws allow anyone to sell ammunition to any one other than a convicted felon. No license or record keeping is required Unlike retailers, ammunition manufactorers need a license, obtained from the ATF for just 10$ a year More disconcerting to the companies is a proposed 50% percent tax on most ammunition sales Competitive pricing already limits profits Thus, premium ammutive pricing already limits profits Thus, premium ammuitives such as the erst while black Talon is precious to bullet makers packaged in boxes of 20, and selling for no less than boxes of 50 regular cartridges typically 15$ to 20$ the premium lines spin big profits which explains why Black Talons equally destructive competitors remain on store shelves while manufactures lie low.

Ban hand gun all Together -

Many city threwout north Amerca has decide to ban gun all together. City such as the district of Columbia, Oakland CA and moor. Feel there city will be a safe place without handgun. Banding of hand Gun have been tryed before in other part of the world with Great success. All hand guns should be banned, from private people, with the exeption of the police Exception to a gun ban would be rifles, and shotguns used by hunters, skeet shooters, and members of target-shooting clubs, and antiques owned by dealers, and collectors. But all weapons would be registered and all owners licensed, with permits renewed on an annual basis subject to an applicant's fitness to hold a permit there should be an amnesty period during which stolen, or unregistered weapons could be handed in without crimination. The government would buy the remaining guns, and destroy them. Yes such a programwould be expensive and complicated to administer it would require yet another snarl of bureaucracy But it could be done, and it would work as smoothly as any other form of registration works once the machinery was in place Ban all handguns is a Idea which time has come.

No Gun in the hand of a person under the age of 21

No one under the age of 21 should be allowed to own a gun. Statistic show most homicede are people who are young-between the age of (19-24) If gun are taking out of this age group hand. The murder rates in the united state should go down. Yes I firmly beleve know one under the age of 21 should own any type of Gun.

These are my personaly, veiws to the solution of gun control. Million of American may not agree with me on the Issue of Guns. But we all know The united state has a serious problem with Gun, and we need some retical approach to this age problem. Which wont go away in the near future.

The Future of Gun Control -

Gun control has become as a crimonious as the brawl over abortion. we are witnessing a clash of absolutes, a struggle between the Quality of life, and a fundamental liberty. It is a debate that has become ossified. On one side are The people who want no control of gun, and on another side of the coin there are people who want some control. With Gun manufactures manufacturing 15,000 new guns a day. And The Goverment is process 10,000 new gun permits per day for anyone wants one. Ans with strong lobby groups sounds the NRA I dont see any changes with The Gun Issue In The near future.

Conclusion -

There is no doubt by now that more guns means more violence Either we stop it now, or this insane domestic arms race will continue. The eidence clearly shows that guns do not protect individuals as much as they endanger society With drive by shooting and the like. The Gun Issue is the only Issue finnal Since 1995 guns have killed more americans than all our enemies have accounted for in all the battle

We ever fough In all the wars combined

was hand Gun killings

100 people In The UK Great brinten

13 In Sweden

95 In Germany

10 In Astralia

68 In Granda

and 20,000 In The United Statements

Gun dont kill people People kill people

God bless Amerca

finnal as for back as the abraham lincoln assantion In 1865 Threw the time of president John F kenndy assantion In 1963 and seanter robert kenndy in 1968 and The Martian Luther king killing The same year and the Malcom X killing In 1965 During the turbulace of the 1960s Guns were the soul cause of these death and more then 95 percent

Hand Guns were used it is high time as we as a society can move into more important issue in owr lives beside The Gun issue in ameca.

The death penalty debate-Another important debate facing the united state today is the death penty debate for offender is prefered to the 3 strike and youre outfed that is about To law in all 50 state in this section we will look at the death penalty as a whole The begin of the death pennlty center over Public oppion age and race of most death peanlty victem goverment in state role in the death peanty debate is the death peanlty a deted to crime conclusion The beginning of the death pennlty debate The death penalty was widly accepted at the time the usantition and th bill constitution is found in the fifth amendment.

The Death peanlty Debate

which reads No person shall be held to answer for a capital, or otherwise infamous crime, unless The crime cane be proving without, reasable doubt. Many stae have used thes consept to deside many high profile cases. One state in particular, which canged many concepts about the death peanlty is the sate of Georgia In 1972, the supreme Court handed down a decision in the death penalties cases of Furman vs Georgia Jackson V Georgia and Branch V Texas, Each of the three defendants had been convicted and sentenced to death Furman for murder, Jackson and Branch for rape In a long confusing desision with nine seperate opinions, and no true majority position, five of the justices held that in the three cases before them the death penalty was cruel and unusual. Justice Marshall and Brannan concluded that the death penalty was totally impermissible The cheif Justice, and Justices Powell Rehnquist, and blackman dissented in separate opinions The majority of five did not hold that capital punishment was in and of itself cruel, and unusual. They held that the way in which the punishment was inflicted on the three defendants in the cases before the coort was cruel and unusual They also argued that the death penalty was so seldom imposed that when itwas imposed it was imposed in a disoriminatory fashion.

In 1976, the US supreme Court reviewed the new death penlty statutes of Georgia, Florida and Texas In the 1984 California death penalty Court Quoted their 1976 Jurek, V Texas decision in affirming the death penalty procedures used by California Texas capital sentencing procedures, like thoe of Georgia and Florida do not violate the Eighth, and Fourteeth Amendments by narrowing its definition of capital murder. Texas has essentially said that there mut be at least one statutory aggravation curcumstance in a fist-degree murder case before a death sentence may even be considered by authorizing the defense to bring before the jury at the separate sentencing hearing whatever mitigation circumstances relating to the individual defendant can be adduced, Texas has ensured that the sentencing jury will have a dequate guidance to enable it to perform its sentencing function by providing by providing prompt judicial review of the jurys decision in a court with state wide jurisdiction Texas has provided a means to promote the even handed, rational, and consistent imposition of death sentences under law. Because this system serves to assure that ssentences of death will not be wantonly, or freakisly imposed, it does not violate the constitution In sum, we cannot say that the judgment of the Georgia legislature that capital punishment may be neccessary in some cases is clearly wrong. Considerations of federalismas well as respect for the ability of legislature to evaluate, In terms of its particular state, the moral consensus concerning the death penalty and its social utility as a sanction, require us to conclude, in the absence of more convincing evidence, that the infliction of death as a punishment for murder is not without justification, and thus is not unconstitutionally severe Finally, we must consider whether the punishment of death is disproportionate in relation to the crime for which it is imposed There is no Question that death as a punishment is unique in its severity, and irrevocable when a dendants life is at stake, the Court has been particularly sensitive to insure that every safeguard is observed. But we are concerned here only with the imposition of capital punishment for the crime of murder, and when a life has been taken deliberately by the offender, we cannot say that the punishment is invariabley disproportionate to the crime It is an extreme sanction, surtable to the most extreme of crimes we hold that the death penalty is not a form of punishment that may never be imposed regaurdless of the offender, and regardless of the procedure followed in reaching the decision to impose it

Public Opionion of the Death peanlty - There been wide fluctuations in the public attitude toward the death penalty in the united states as reflected in public opinion polls the percentage of respondents favoring the death penalty since 1933 The rise in proportion of death penalty advocates may be due to the conservation backlash of the 970s Characteristics believed to be associatedwith the formation of a favorable attitude toward capital punishment incclude being older, being better educated, being more affuent, being white fearing being victimized, and believing the effecacy of punishment when one examines social psychology attributes, supporters of the death penalty are frequently found to be authoritarian, practices and excessive intrafamily violence Obvioussly, on can support the death penalty for a variety of reasons and causes. The states without the death penalty prior to (Furman vs Georgia)

State	Date Abolished
Rhode Island	1852
Wisconsin	1853
Maine	1887
Minnesota	1911
North Dakota	1915
Hawaii	1958
Alaska	1957
Michigan	1963
Oregon	1964
Iowa	1965
West Virginna	1965
Vermont	1965
New York	1965

Percentage of Amercan who support the death Penalty

60% for the death penalty

30% against

18% undeide

2% dont care

Clearly the death penalty is alive and well in the streets without any of the nagiative initation plaed by the courts Many who oppose the life sentence as a replacment for the death penalty observe that the parol laws in many states make it posible for a lifer to get out in a relatively breif time, usually those who receive life sentences become eligible for parole in therteen years The proposed answer to this argument is to remove the hope of parole from a life sentence. but this action would constitute an admission that certain prisonerss could not be rehabilitated and would destroy the offenders possible incentive to change their behavior patterns. The chance that tan innocent persson might be convicted also detracts from the acceptability of th irreversible life sentence.

<u>Age of most death peanlty Inmate</u> - The average age of most death peanlty Inmate are between 24 and 44. Most of these Inmate are located in souther state. Mostly in the state of florida and Georgia, and Texas

<u>Race of most death peanalty Inmate</u> - one frequent and continuous argument against capital punishment Equability is basially concerned with the disproportionate infliction of capital punishment against minorities those with court oppinted counsel, males, immigrant the young, and members of lower classes The Issue are fundamental fairness and equal protection under the Constitution strong evidence exists that the death penalt is invoked in a discriminating fachion In a study of florida as death-row inmates, researches unearthed evidence that he race of the victim also influences the imposition of the death penalty. Not one white person on death row who killed only a single victim killed a black person The data for all 83 offenders while the researchers are careful not to claim that such racial discrimination definitely exists, The evidence implies that this remains a troubling issue requiring further study

Florida Death Row Inmates by Race of offender and Victims killed note period 1988 To19900 Data

Perpetrators	Victims (white)	Black
White	52	1
Black	46	7
Other	6	0

As you can see black in the state of Florida are over represent on death row. Black in most other state are also our represented on death row. Mostly in the South

Goverment and state role in the Death peanlty Debate

State - As method early, state vary on there desions of the death peanalty. By the end of 1980s 37 states Had Death Penalty Laws in Effect of the more than 3,800 executions that have occurred Since 1930

86% percent were for murder

60% percent took place in the south

76% percent occurred before 1950

More than 53 percent of those executed were black

Less than 1 percent of those executed were female.

In the 1972 land mark case of fuman v Georgia the US Sepreme Court ruled that the death penalty as applied in the various states of ten had been used in an arbitrary, and capricious manner there by violating Eight Amendment guarantees against cruel, and unusual punishment All of the more than 600 person then living on death row eventually had their capital sentences removed. However, the numbers began to build up again as many state moved Quickly to revise their capital punishment laws. All and all the desition of death peanalty in the 37 state which the death peanlty is allowed depends on jude, and jury and the state supreme courts justice in those states - So in simmary although there are no exact figures available, we know that thousands of muders, and rapes are committed annually in the states where death is an authorized punishment for those crimes Informed selectivity, of couse, is a value not to be denigrated yet presumably the states could make precisely the same claim if there were 10 executions per year of five, or even if there were but one That there may be as many as 50 per year docs not strengthen the claim when the rate of infliction is at this low level it is highly implausible that only the worst criminals or the criminals who commit the worst crimes are selected for this punishment No one has yet suggested a rational basis that could differentiate in those terms the few who die from the many who go to prison crimes, and criminals simple do not admit of a distintion that can be drawn so finely as to explain, on that ground, the execution of such a tiny sample of those eligible Certainly the laws that provide for this punishment do not attempt to draw that distinction all cases to which the laws apply are necessarily extreme Nor is the distinction credible in fact If for example petitioner Furman, or his crime illustrate the extreme them nearly all murderers and their murders are also extreme Futher more, our procedures in death cases, rather than resulting in the selection of extreme cases for this punishment, actually sanction an arbitrary selective For this court has held that juries may, as they do, make the decision whether to impose a death sentence wholly unguided by standards governing that desision Mc (Gautha v California) 402 U.S. 183, 196-208, 915 ot 1454, 1461-1468 28 LED2d 711 1971 In other words our procedures are not constructed to guard against the totally capricious selection of criminal for the punishment of death.

Goverment Role in the death peanlty Debate - There is no perfect procedure for deciding in which cases governmental authority should be used to Impose death vary depending on on crimes commited and by who three of the most common crimes were the goverment may strongly earge the death peanlty would be (4) Terrism

(1)treson

(2)airptracy - Congress enacted 1974 In 35 states

(3)dissent -

Treson - has been found in every greater is in Amercan history Benedict Arnold, Aaron burr, the copperhead movement the fifth column, and Alger Hiss all played a part in the history of treason Yet until the

Roseberg in the 1950. No Ameerican was ever executed for treason only a handful have died as traitors until world war II every convicted traitor Included those who deserted the army during tie of war received a presidential pardon.

Airpiracy - Most country in the world consider, high jacking one of the most serious crime today. Our goverment has also made high jacking a crime ponishable be death. fortunaly owr goverment has not Executed any one for this crime.

Dissent - Dispite the First amendment guarantees to right of dissent, the amount of dissent to be tolerated has never been made completey clear. In resoned years, disent is growing in all segment of society toward the goverment on a variety of Issue. The most widly know Aisent in the 1990s is the insedent involving a religious cult in Waco Texas, were member of the of a sect lead by david corese disagreed with govement And Goverment rules and regulation

(4)Terrisim - we all are very aware Ther events of all which is still freash in all of our minds Terrism is The must protand issue facing America Today Terrisem is surver of crime it is pushable by Death The united states goverment has placed Terresim The number one Threat To The united states Today and as you can see why The war in To make Terrisem a thing of The Past and This is one wat we must win more about Terreism in later chapter.

also 1995 there was a number of disent toward the goverment. a boming in the City Oaklahoma City Which Cost Over 150 lives Is the strongest show of disent in the 1990s Timmy Mcvay, and Terry Nichal are the two people who were the crime suspects of the crime. And the goverment seeked the death peanlty In that case. Ther eis no perfect procedure for deciding in which cases governmental authority should be used to impose death But a statute that prevents the sentence in all capital cases from giving independent mitigating weight to aspects of the defendants character and record, and to cicumstances of the offense proffered in mitigation creates the risk which may call for a less severe penalty when the choice is between life, and death that risk is unacceptable, and imcompatible with the commands of the eighth and fourteeth Amendments.

Is the death peanlty a deterred to crime - Statistical attempts to evaluate the worth of the death penalty as a deterrent to crimes by potential offenders have occasioned a great deal of debate. The results simple have been inconclusive although some of the studies suggest that the death penalty may not function as a significantly greater deterrent than lesser penalties there is no coavinoing empicical evidence either supporting, or refuting this veiw. The death penalty is said to serve two principals social purposes retribution and deterrence of capital crimes by prospective offenders. In part, capital punishment is an expression of societys moral outrage at particularly offensive conduct This function may be unappealing to many, but it is essential in an ordered society that asks its citizens to rely on legal processes rather than self help to vendicate their wrongs.Finally, we must consider whether the punishment of death is disproprtinate in relation to the crime for which it is imposed There is no question that death as a punishment is unique in its severity, and irrevocability when a defendants life is at stake, the Court has been particularly sensitive to insure that every safeguard is observed. But we are concerned here only with the imposition of capital punishment for the crime of murder, and when a life has been taken deliberately by the offender, we cannot say that the punishment is invariably disprotionate to the crime It is an extreme sanction, suitable to the most extreme of crimes. We hold that the death penalty is not a form of punishment that may never be imposed, regardless of the circumstances of the offenses, regardless of the character of the offender, and regardless of the procedure followed in reaching the decision to impose it.

Conlusion - Other country are using other methods To deter criminals. China, which has excuted 20,000 criminal In the past 10 years between (1990-2000) for varisy reasons. rape, murder ect. Are Televising there excutions to the public. So they can see the reality of death. And with 3,000 people in owr country on death row across the country. Many feel televised exections is the best way to deter criminal of the future. Critics say televised excution places no privacy on the person being excuted. All in all the debates will continue for many many years to come.

<u>Drug relationship to the crime problem -</u>

Ever serious study of crime in this country point to drug profits as the main cause of criminal behavyor Excluding outlays for police protection, and incarceration, drug abuse in america levies costs on society in the form 40 billion dollar annually. In this section we will look at the drug problem as a whole. The beginning of the drug problem what are The drugs of chose. Alchohol relatinship to the crime problem. The state role to the drug problem, The Goverment role In the drug problem. some solution to the drug problem. Conclusion

<u>The begginning of drugs</u> - The use of drugs, whether to achieve relaxation and pleasure or to treat illness has long been part of the human condition. Yet it is only within the past century, or so that drug addiction and abuse have been regarded major social problems Although governments have attempted to criminalize various aspects of the use possession, or sale of drugs there are substantial numbers in the population who continue their drug-consuming habits in violation of the criminal law The specifics of drugs use, and abuse are complex in part because of the tremendous scientific advances over the past several decades

It is especially Interesting to note that rates of drug use have remained high, and continued to increase despite law enforccement efforts The number of arrests for drug violations has increased dramatically Between 1965 and 1969 the increase was six fold. There was a subsequent doubling between 1970 and 1980 with the result that in 1980 there were more than 550,000 arrests for drug violations Most of these arrests appear to involve cannabis Neverless it is possible that patterns of drug use may change although drug use has remained widespread, there were some modest declines in recent years The declines were attributed to factors such as growing concern about health risks among the young mounting disapproval of peers, and the changing mood of the times, rather than to control the supply through rigorous law enforcement

<u>What are the drug of choice</u> - There are many drugs on the market for a varity of people I will place emphasis on the 3 major drugs (which are Illegal) but in high demand They are

(1) marijuana -

(2) Herion -

(3) Coain -

<u>Marijuana</u> - One drug heavily used by million of American is the drug called marijuana, Originally, its use had been largely confined to the Mexican community, and some Native American groups. But since 1960 there has been an immense increase in the number of users. Now estimated at anywhere from 5 million to 20 million users of marijuana Included many middle class adolescents and young adults. They are typically found on high school, and college campuses estimates are that 20 to 50 percent of high school, and college students have tried marijuana a few times, and perhaps one-third of those who have tried it continue to use it occasionally, or regularly marijuana use in the 1960s had a distrnut age factor those under 25 were far more likely than those over 25 to have tried it often its use in and of itself was symbolic of protest against the establishment.

<u>Dependence of marijuana and comprared to other drugs</u> -

Marijuana differs from other drugs such as cocain, herion ect includes no physical dependence, and is most often consumned in intimate groups For many users, it represents primary deviance in that they typically carry on an otherwise normal life. Yet at the same time, it involves participation in groups that are often antagonistic to establish socciety. Secondarydeviance for the marijuana user appears to be a function of having contact with many users which increases the likelihood of becoming a seller. This in turn increases the isolation from the convential world. The result is assuming the role of secondary deviant.

<u>Marijuana based on age of user</u> - Most marijuana user are young between the age of 16 To 20. Most of these users state out using marijuana In high school or junner high. Do to high presure from peir group. Most

young people start out using the drug for fun. Heavy Research has shown Marijuana is not adictive after long use.

Location of most Marijuana user - Most marijuana user are located In large metroplitan coty In the northern part of the country. According to many observers, There are also thousnad of marijuana user located in rural America mostly in the southern part of the united state as well.

Black males - Black males who use marju, and are usually young age (18-23) Most black male who use marijuana are mostly located In souther citys. After age 24 the use of marajuana for black males decrease.

Black females - Blak females who use marijuana are also young between the age of (17-22) Most black female who use marijuana are located in large metroplations city in the eastern part of the united states. After age 22 marijuana use by black females level off

White Males - White male who use marijuana are once again young between the age of (18-23) most white male who use the drug are located in the western part of the united state. White male are the number once consumer of marijuana over all other genders. After age 23 the consumuption of marijuana by white male level off.

White females - White female who use marijuana are also young The average age of most white female marijuana smokers is around (17-20) Most white female who smoke marijuana are located In eastern coty. After the age 21 marijuana smoked by white females levels off. Finnal marijuana is a drug which has been used for hundreds of years. Over that period of time researchs have found marijuana serve many purposes. One secnifcant purpose Is the use of marijuana has been use to help locoma patient live longer and better lives. This Is one Illegal drug million of brrercan, Included myself. Strongly feel sould be legallyed. Many Goverment official feel Legallaiztion of marijuana is not to far down the road. Many beleive this is one drug which will do more good than harm.

Herion - The third widly illegal drug used in the united state is the drug called Herion. There are believed to be over 1 million Herion atticks in the united states. Most of these attics are located on the Eastcoast. One city in particular New York. Which has over 300,000 attics along. In this section we will look at the beginning of the growth of Herion in owr country, and Herion use by race, location of most user, And herion in the future.

The beginning of Herion in the united states - The use of herion began, In the united state over a hundred years ago. People back then, used the drug for a varitey of reason. Doctors used the drug to help them with complicated surgerys. Layman used Herion to get high off the drugs. Sence then herion use have grown tenfold. At one time, the herion market was supplied almot totally by poppies grown in Turkey In fact, while one part of Turkey"s poppy crop went for illegal herion, the other was sold to pharmaceutical companies for conversion to medicinal morphine. The illegal opium was shipped to france, and corsica, where it was converted to herion cut, and shipped to the united states.

Perhaps less there is enormous dilution as the narcotics go from the poppy field to the addict Opium is harvested with the poppies, morphine is extracted from the opium, and then converted to herion. Then the heroin is cut by adding powders of similar color, and consistency packaged into capsules, and solf to the sonsumer. The dilution is such that an estimated 5 tons of pure herion is suffecient to supply the entire addict population of the united stat for one years. Whatever the source, the reported profit in illegal herion is enormous when opium wass sold at 25 per kilogram, the cost of the raw materials in a New York City bag of heroin was about one-fourth of a cent Obviously this implies immense profits, but there are also intermediaries along the way Aide from the foreign exporters there are importers rarely addicts themselves professional whosalers are rarely addicts peddlers or retailers who may be addicted, and pushers addicts who sell to get funds for their own drug supplies from the original importer reach 4320 addicts one most interesting feature of this organization is that it functions extremely well on a continuous basic despite police interference, and despite adsence of extensive contact or communication among people on different levels of the distrubution system.

<u>Age of most Herion users</u> - The average age of most herion user is between 21 To 44. Most user state using herion after trying other drugs such as cocain speed ect.

<u>Location of most Herion user.</u> Most Herion user are located In large mereopoliton city on the east cost. There are also many Herion user located In large metroplatain city on the west cost.

<u>Herion use based on raise</u>

<u>White male</u> - Who use the Illegal drug Herion are middle age between 30 and 40 years old. White male consume the drug herion more so than any other gender. Most of these white males who use The drug are located on the east cost city like New york, Philidelheia Boston and Baltimoer. Most of the white male who consume the drug are locates in these cotys.

<u>White females</u> - White female who use the drug Herion are in there mid 30s to early 40s most white female who use herion are located in large metropolitan citys on the west cost. There is estimated to be over 100,000 white female on herion in 4 major city in California, Los Anglese, Oakland, Sanfrancisco and San Diego.

<u>Black male on herion</u> - Black male on herion are mistly in there mid 30s to mid 40s. Most black male who use the drug are located in southern coty, and easter cotys. Ther eis estimate to be nearly 500,000 black male who use the drug on a dailey bases.

<u>Black female</u> - Black female, who usse the Illegal drug herion Are also in there mid 30 To mid 40s most black female who use the Illegal drug herion are located in large cities on the east cost. There is estimate to be two hundred thousand. black female who use the drug herion on a dailey basis, threw out the country. finnal herion is conceded to be a hard drug. And use of this drug over a period of time will lead to sever Health problem. Herion is one drug which sould be regulated very careful by geverment, and state health offical This is one drug which sould not be in the hands of a laymen. This drug has cost thousand of

lives over the years. And if goverment and world leaders dont stop the spread of herion. There will be more lives lost in the near future.

Cocain - In todays world The drug of choice is crack cocain The use of this drug has exploded over the past 15 years. People from all walks of live use this drug on a dailey bases. In this section we will look at the beginning of the use of cocain who are the highest user of the drug. were are the most user of the Drug located. Black cocain, use white coain use and conclusion.

The beginning of cocain use in America - Cocain use was stated Back around the turn of the century. Back then the drug was used as a ingredient of medicines and soft drinks sence then million of people have used the drug to get a high.

Cocain use based on age . Most cocain user are in there mid twenties, and early 30s.Most of these cocain user started using other drugs before using cocain. Drug such as speed marijuana in the likes Are drug tryed Before using Cocain.

Cocain use based on location = Most cocain user are located In large metropolatin city in the Northeast. There are many also located in rural commuties threwout the united states

Cocain based on race

Black male - Black males who use cocain are usually around there mid 20s and early 30s. Most black males who use the drug. Are located in southern city. It is estimate that over 3 million black male use cocain on a daily bases. Threw out the united state.

Black female - Black female who use the drug cocaine are in The lower econimic bracket usely under 10,000 years. Most black female who use crack cocain are single parent mother In large metropolitain city all across the united state. Most black female who use the drug are between the age of 25 To 44. It is estimate that 2 million black female use the drug on a dailey bases Most of these black female are located In large city on the east cost.

<u>White males</u> - White males who use the Illegal Drug cocain are mostly in there late 20s to mid 40s. Most white males who use cocain are in the higher Income brancket White male use cocain more so than any other gender. Some white male have used the drug with a combination of herion, which is commonly knew as speedballing. White males who use cocain are mostly Located in large citys on the west cost. it is estimate that over 11 million white male use cocain on a daily bases.

<u>Conclusion</u> - Cocain is one drug drug dealer cant keep in stock these days. And with the epidemic of the cocain crazy of today. Cocain in starting to effected million of Americans. Cocain is another drug which should not be used by a layperson. With 43% of all death in amerca caused by Heart failure oain. used Imprperly may speed up the heart, and may kill. With billions of dollars ar stake threwout the world wide Illegal drug trade. I dont see any reason why a few lives lost will stop this billion dollar a year Illegal business In the near future.

<u>Alcoholism to the crime problems -</u> Alcoholism cost the united states 6 billion in medical expenses 25 billion lost wages and 79 billion as a result of pain and suffering endured by individuals Alcoholism effected all Income level, and all genders. In this section we will look at the begging of alcoholism in America Alcoholism based on age, location, race, conclusion

<u>The beginning of alcoholism in Amecar</u> - Use of alcohol is an old American tradition, brought over by the early colonists In the early days, most alcohol was consumed in the form of beer and wine. But by the late 1700s about 90 percent of the alcohol consumed was in the form of distilled spirits. However, this percentage dropped as later European immigrants brought their national drinking customs with them, and by the 1900s There was consumption of all three form of alcohol. Drinking has been wide spread in American society-one estimate of the average consumption is 2.65 gallons per year for each American 15 years or older-and today is commonly practiced on numerous social occasions More over, this parcapite figure does not reflect the fact that since many Americans do not drink at all these who do drink consume significantly greater amounts of alcohol In light of the wide spread

consumption, and public acceptance of alcohol, it is remarkable that the united states is the only industrial country that has ever attempted to go cold turkey and totally prohibit its use Neverthless Prohibition was enacted in 1920, in the Eighteenth Amendment. to the constitution plus some related laws, which mode it Illegal to mawufactures, consume or sell alcohol beverages. Prohibition posed many problems and was relatively short lived. Rigorous abstinence conflicted directly with well-established drinking patterns, so that evasion of the law was widespread. Thousands of speakeasies Illigal drinking establishments-accommodated the drinking public Police curruption was encouraged. organized crime received a great impetus, since it moved in to provide much desired but illegal liquor Repeal came in 1933 in the form of another constitutional amendment, the Twenty-First Amendment Since adults-although the details of the laws differ from state to state. Although the repeal of Probibition gave recognition to the unworkability of a law. Which ran counter to widespread practice, certain behaviors related to drinking have continued to be criminalized. For the mosst part criminalization has concentrated on public behavior related to drinking driving under the Influence of alcohol Which can have very serious consequences. Violation of liquor laws, and drunkenness in public continue to be crimes. In fact, although there has been some decline in recent years these three offenses still account for more than one out of every four police arrests. In addition, many of the arrests for disorderly conduct, vagrancey, and violations of curfews, and loitering laws may also involve alcohol-related behavior. Many alcoholics are primary deviants who attempt to maintain normality in the other aspects of their life Yet secondary deviance related to alcohol can be seen in those who frequent the skid rows of American cities

Alcohlism based on age - Most alcoholics are located all across America. Most alcohlics are located In large metroplotion city. Most of these alcohlics are located In city In the south and southwest.

Alchlics based on race

White males - White male who are alcohlics are between the age of 40 To 60s. White male over represent all other gender of alcoholics do to shape number of them. most white male who are alcohlics are In the high Income bracket. Do to job stress, and home Infiement many white male turn to alcohol over Illegal drugs. Most white males who are alcohlic are located In the south, and southwest part of the united states. Where there is beleved to be more then 300,000 white male alcohlics located there.

White females - White female who are alcohlics are between the age of 35 To 55. Most white female who are alcohlics are usally married. with 2 to 3 children, and living in the subera. Most of these white female are located. In the midwest were there is estimated to be 100,000 or more white female alcoholics.

Black male alcoholics - black male alcohlics are between the age of 45 To 60 most of these black male are In The middle income bracket The majority of these black male ar elocated in the south were there is believe to be 2 million black Male between the age of 45 To 60 who are alcohol

Black female - black female who are alcohlic are between the age of 35 To 45. Most of these black female are single and are In The lower, Income bracket. Most of these black female are located In the eastern city of the united states.

Conclusing - There is as yet no know generally effective method for treating the vast number of alcoholics in our society. Some individual alcoholics have responded to a particular forms of therapy with remissions of their symptomatic dependence upon the drug But just as ther eis no agreement among doctors and social workers with respect to the causes of alcoholism, there is no consensus as to why particular treatment have been effective in particular cases, and there is no generally agreed-upon approach to the problem of treatment on a large scale. Most pscychiatrists are apparently of the opinion that aloholism is far more difficult to treat than other forms of behavioral means of psychiatrists In particular, have been seveerely criticised for the prevailing relucctance to undertake the treatment of drinking problems Thus it is entirely possible that even were the manpower, and facilities available for a full-scale attack upon chronic alcoholism, we would find ourselves unable to help the vast bulk of out visible-let along our invisible alcoholic population. However, facilities for the attempted treatment of indigent aloholics are woefully lacking throughout the country. It would be tragic to return large numbers of helpless, sometimes dangerous, and frequently unsanitary inebriates to the streets of our cities without even the opportunity to sober up adequately which a brief jail term provides Presumably no state, or city will tolerate such a state of affairs. Yet the medical profession cannot, and does not, tell us with any assurance that, even If the buildings, equipment and trained personnel were made available, it could provide anything more than slightly higher class jail for our indigent habitual inebriates. Thus we run the grave risk that nothing will be accomplished byond the hanging of a new sign-reading hospital- over one wing of the jail house.

States and Goverments role in the drug problem - The state and The federal Goverment both have there own idea on fighting the drug problem of today. In this section we will look at both. first states.

State A state might impose criminal sanctions for example, against the unauthorized manufacture, prescription, sale, purchase, or possession of narcotics within its border. In the interest of dicouraging the violation of such laws, or in the interest of the eneral health, or welfare of its inhabitants a state might establish program of compulsary treatment for those addicted to narcotics such a program of treatment might require periods of involuntary confinement And penal sanctions might be imposed for failure to comply with established compulsary treatment procedures, or a statemight shoose to attack the evil of narcotics traffic on broader fronts also through public health education for example, or by efforts to ameliarate the economic and social conditions under which those evils might be thought to flourish. In short the range of valid choices which a state might make in this area is undoubtedly a wide one, and the wisdom of any particular chouce within the allowable spectrum is not for us to decide. This statute, therefore, is not one which punishes a person for use of narcotics, for their purchase, sale or possession, or for anti social, or disorderly behavior resulting from their administation It is not a law which even pueports to provide, or require

111

medical treatment rather we deal with a statute which makes the status of narcotic addiction a criminal offense, for which the offender may be prosecuted "at anytime before he reforms. The addict is a sick person the may of course, be confined for treatment or for the protection of society. Cruel and unusual punishment results not from confinement but from convicting the addict of a crime. The purpose of (1721) is not to cure, but to penalize were the purpose to cure, there would be no need for a mandatory jail term of not less than 90 days. A prosecution for addiction with its resulting stigma, and irreparable demage to the good name of the accused, cannot be justified as a means of protecting society where a court commtment would do as well Indeed In 5350 of the welfare and Institutions Code, California has expressly provided for ovill proceedings for the commitment of habitual addicts sections 1721 is in reality, a direct attempt to punish those the state cannot commit civilly. This prosecution has no realation to the curing of an Illness Indeed, it cannot, for the prosecution is aimed at penalizing an illness, rather than at providing medical care for it we would forget the teahings of the Eight Amendment If we allowed sickness to be made a crime, and permitted sick people to be punished for being sick This age of enlightenment cannot to lerate such barbarous action. The statute must first be placed in perspective. California has a comprehensive and enlightened program for the control of narcoticism based on the overriding policy of prevention, and cure apart from prohibiting specific acts such as the purchase, possession, and sale of narcotics. California has taken certain legislative steps in regard to the status of being a "narcotic addict"-a condition commonly recognized as a threat to the state and to the individual The code deals with this problem in realistic stages At its incipleney narcotic addiction is handled under Sect 11721 of the health, and saftey Code which is at issue here. It provides that a person found to be addicted to the use of narcotics shall serve a term in the county jail of not less than 90 days no more than one year with the minimum 90-day confinement apply in all cases without exception provision is mafe for parole with periodic tests to detect readdiction. There was no suggestion that the term narcotic addictsas used in sact 11721 included a person who acted without volition or who had lost the power to self-control Although setion is penal In appearance perhaps a carry-over form a less sophisticated approach-it present provisions are Quite similar to those for civil commitment and treatment of addicts who have lost the power of self control where narcotic addiction has progressed beyond the inicipient, volitional stage, California provides for commitiment of three mouths to two years in a state hospital California welfare, and Istitutions Code Sect 5355 for the purpose of this provision, a narcotic addict is defined as any person who habitually takes, or other wise uses to the extend of having lost the power of self-control any opium morphine, cocain or other narcotics drug. Thus, the criminal provision applies to the incipient narcotic addict who retains self-control, requirring confinement of three mouths to one year and a parole with frequent tests to detect renewed use of drugs Its overriding purpose is to cure the less seriously addicted person by preventing futher use. On the other hand the civil commitment provision deals with addicts who have lost the power of self-control, requiring hospitalization up to two years. Each deals with a different type of addicts. But with a common purpose This is mot apparent when the sections overlap if after civil commitment of an addicts it is found that hospital treatment will not be helpful, the addict is confined for a minimum period of three months in the same manner as is the volitional addict under the criminal provision. State might establish a program of compulsary treatment for those addicted to narcotics which might require periods of involuntary confinement I submit that California has done exactly that. The majoritys error is In instructing the California Legislature that hospitalization is the only treatment for narcotics addiction-that anything less is a punishment denying due process. California has found otherwise after a study which I suggest was more extensive than that conducted by the court. The fact that Sect. 11721 might be labled criminal seems irrelevant, not only to the majority's own treatment test but to the conept of ordered liberty to which the states must attain under the Fourteenth Amendment The test is the overally purpose and effect of a state's act and I submit that California's program relative to narcotic addicts-including both the criminal and "civil" provisions-is inherently one of treatment and lies well within the power of the state.

Many staes are using California Drug treatment program In there state To stop the spread of drug abuse in there city, and commuity. Many feel California drug Policy laws are a protecal of exellence which should be used as a example across the country

Goverment role in the drug problem   The united state goverment has used a variitey of method to stop the spread of illegal Drug over the years One of the most important piece of federal legislation the goverment has passed was the hairison act of 1914. The Hairison act was originally designed as a piece of federal legislation responding to international pressure to establish systems for internal control of narcotics, and to concern over to many addicts It required only that addicts obtain drugs from physiians registered under the act, and that records be maintained. However, subsewuent court interpretations drastically restricted the discretion of doctors to prescribe opiates In the process, the act also became interpreted as a tax measure, and the Treasury Department become entrusted with its enforcement Implementation of the Harrison act, and its subsequent interpretations made an enormous difference in the pattern of drug use in the united stae by 1920 The Social characteristics of the users had begun to change from female, middle-aged, and middle-class to male, young, and poor, or minority. For another, the continuing drug traffic became tainted with criminality. Some doctors who continued to prescribe drugs for their addicted patients were put into prison Professional criminals, and organized crime, operation on an international scale took control over the drug traffic Law enforcement showed sign of corruption.

other drug legislation - The repeal of prohibition meant that drugs other that alcohol became the center of national policy In a sense, enforcement of narcotics prohibition filled the moral void left when alcohol prohibition ended In deed it is worth nothing that the Education of Parent To the drug problem of owr young people. formal adoult education, schooling after work classes on fundamental social problems, raising a new patriotim that adresses the internal dangers in America of the drug problem of owr young is essential Most parent dont knew there children are using Illegal drug with Parent course, and education about illegal drugs will help Parents cope with there children on a one on one bases. These course have helped thousand of Parents related to there children drug problem and have a understanding of why they chose to use Illegal drug In the first place.

legalizing of drug - Is legalizing drugs an answer? Me personally I dont advocate leglization, but people who feel legalizing is the answer have'nt noticed, or perhaps won't admit that the flood gates were pushed open years ago to addiction is created by a number of conditions, but availability of drugs only threw a doctors prescrption Drugs doctors can legilize prescribed would be marijuana, Quaalude legalization is not the answer to a age old problem. Which may take years of debate before socety as a whole is ready to exept a clear cut veiw on this mater.

Selective arrests to go after drug dealers. - Spend less money or, rather, save the enormous sum we now spend-on futile drug busts in the streets Spend more money interdicting the drug invasion use military forces, and use special forces and millitary intelligence in high drug area. After all street drug dealers are the small potates in the billion dollar drug war. Society wants the big boys in this war on drugs Not the corner drug dealer.

Federal narcotics bureau was created in 1930 Just as poshibition was coming to an end, so that there could be more coopetive law enforcement between federal, and local office at the same time the bureau also difined, and shared the cut line of the drug problem. 28 billion dollor crime bill - In 1994 congress passed one of the largest anti drug legizaotin in history is to give drug dealer longer sentence with position, or sell of crack cocain. This disition has let to several Federal Prison up rising In 1995 In the midwest. By Inmate who are In prison for Drug relate crime. Many feel the sdesition is to harsh a treatment to human being who are sick, and need treatment. Then to be locked up for 20 to 30 years. or live Finnal, Feederal laws on mandatory sentene is flawed and distract, with lots of contribution. Tobacco is a drug yet the tabacco industry is allowed to promote smokeing through print, and bill board advertising. And the federal government collects taxes from tobacco sales alcohol is a drug yet commercial a bound on television linking beer consumption to be sexy, and having fun. And the federal goverment collects taxes from beer, wine and liquor sale. The federal law that make growing 100 or more marijuana plants a felony punishmable by a mandatrory five year prison sentene is cruel treatment. Everyone has there own opinion about the federal goverment aproach has there own opinion about the federal goverment aproach on drug policy. For owr postered of the future.

Some Solution to the drug problem

- There has been many suggestion over the year on how to deal with the drug problem facing, or society. Here a endepth veiw of the 5 most popular plan today.

(1)Educate of parents To the drug Problems facing the young people Today

(2)legalizing of drugs.

(3)Selective arrests To go after drug dealers.

(4)neigborhood watch in the community.

(5)Chang some of the feiture laws.

Neigbor hood watch in community were drug are a problem

Many community threwout the united state are starting neigborhood watch program. Groups like wishington Metro, or anger Hall Coplition Videotape street corner drug transaction Members of The Iver Hanks Neigborhood watch in Los Angeles make citizen arrests of drug dealers who try to sell them Illegal drugs. Community watch program has been very successful In many commuty aross the country. And may be sucessful In yours.

forfeiture laws - Are used to take money away from the drug dealers in theory, to remove their motive for selling drugs. many feel we as a society should take another approach. Give drugs to rebilitied users whih removes their incentive to steal to support their habit. In one day every drug pusher is out of business. Many believe forfeiture laws need to be changed. from the top (meaning goverment), and the administations that have proceded ot seem much more intersted in seizure, pursuit, and punishment than in treatment. These approach are retical To many. But if we as a society want to change people about drugs, and the use of them we must come up with retical approach to this age old Problem. And That problem is Illegal Drugs.

Conclusions - Chasing drug dealers from city to city and neibohood to neiborhood. Has cost socety billion of dollors. Socety is tired of the cat, and mouse game are goverment, and states are playing in this war on drugs. People want to see results. Drug abuse is effecting ever major aspect of owr dayly lives. People who get there home broken in to by people looking for money to support their habits. Mugging victims Innocents cought In shoot-outs over drug sales, and turf, every tax payer who pays for this war with money and lost freedoms, and all who have lived in the war. However the drug trade is such that there is no shortage of new candidated. willing to take the place of those drug dealers sent off to prison. Although 60 percent of federal inmates are in jail for drug related crimes, or alcohol related crimes. There has been no noticeble decline in drug dealing. The result of the crackdown on drugs has been carnage in the large metoplation citys. African Americans are the main victems of crime. Being three times more likely to be victem of vilent crimes more so then whites. Do The high drug use among blacks not to methods, The cost of mediccal, and mental health care as well as losst wages, and produtity. Drug reduced the Quality of there lives. And with more drugs on the street then ever before. Citys and statess must take a new approach to win the war on Drugs.

Hundreds of people have giving suggestion of how to solve the crime problem in america. From police to politition and criminalgest. And they all have there own idea, and opionions. Here are a list of my suggestion on how solve crime problem in todays world.

1) Free up more resourse for more people. Especially low Income peoples.

2) Try to stay abreast of whats going on in your community.

3) More job secity higer wadge.

4) Less crime on tv.

5) More respect for one another.

6) More eye, and ears in the community.

7) Tougher court sentence for criminals.

8) More police on the street.

9) More money in major citys.

10) High social programs, in citys were there is high crime rates.

11) Create more wealth Americans.

12) Natinal ID Card.

13) Better tecknology for crime prevention.

1) <u>Free up more resourse for more people.</u>

America is indeed the richest country in the world with a GNP of over 5 trillion per year. Make it more eaiser for the average person to obtain some of this vast wealth in our country. The averge person edcuntional level is only 12 grade, meaning, knowlege is important to obtain wealth, without the expertise of how to become professional wealth is highly unobtainable. We need more goverment involvement to reach the poorest of the poorest. So they can have the knowledge how on how to obtain more resources.

2) <u>Try to stay abreast of whats going on in your community.</u>

By knowing whats going on in your community. You will always be aware of things around you. You do not what to be blind to events were you live. By reading newspapers and trade magazine. You will stay abreast of events dailey keep up with your local news, and raido broadcast, about events which occurs from day to day. On the issue of crime.

3) <u>More job secity, and higer wages.</u>

Work is important to ever human being. Without work bring idealnessbing povety bring trouble; which bring crimes. With more union involment to keep employees on job longer. Will reduce disfrienchment of employees. Who are not happy with there jobs. Union can help fight for higer wadges for low payed employees. Who may be temted to stael, or lye. Which may bring crime on the work place. Full employment in America has never been, and may not ever be. But with more goverment involment, and state programs to help the porr. With job training, and job skills. Will reduce crime in citys were there is high unemployment.

4) <u>Less crime on TV.</u>

Crime in the media still-plays a part. Percentage of americans who think that violence on television programs directly contributes to violence in real life 79% percentage who would support governmental intervention to limit tv violence. TV is the number one meda in the united state. People watch TV more then read newspapers, or listen to the radio. The media(TV) can have a profound effect on million of people views. In how they see the world, and how they reacted toward others around them, with less crime on TV people will see less. And what they don't see wont hurt.

5) <u>More respect for one another.-</u>

We live in a world of stranger. Every person is different with different need, and desire. If we would learn to respect one another views, and opoinon. Then there would be less likely to be conflict between one another. Respect for one another is the most important aspect of our dailey lives.

6) <u>More eye and ears in communty.</u>

Keep your eyes, and ear open for events around you most communty around the united state. Have neiberhood watch programs. These programs have helped in Community were there is high crime rates. With out these programs, meaning community would fall into hand of gangs, and drug dealers. So these programs have helped keep crime low in and were there is high crime rates.

7) <u>Tougher court sentence for criminals.</u>

Court systems in the united state from state to state. And from city to city. Many court system are very lienunited toward criminals who have prior criminal records and most of these criminals are repeat ofenders.

Courts most become more harster twoard criminals, who have been in the system for years, and years. Courts system code.

Associates court AS

County auditor CA

County clears office CH

Circuit court CI

County court of Zbw CL

Concillation court CN

Common claims CP

County court CT

City court CN

District court DC

Domestic court DO

District judge system DS

Federal distric court IE

General session GS

Inferrior court IC

Justice of the peace JU

Magistrate court MA

Municipal court MU

1st magisteral court M1

2nd magisteral court M2

3rd magisteral court M3

Quarterly court MD

Porish court PC

Probation court RR

Recorder of deeds RD

Small claims SC

State court ST

Superior court SU

These are a listing of court system throug out the united state. These listing may very from city to city acording to were you live. And state to state.

8) <u>more police on the streets in high crime areas</u>

For the fifth time since 1984 congress, Has pass major crim ligistation. The most important item likely to emerge from tough barganing between the house, and senate is money for between 50,000 and 100,000 more police officers. Cities will have to pay one forth to one half the cost of each cop. Initially an provide full funding after great buildup in federal law enforcement were finally going to be putting bodies wer their most useful on city street. Let it will take years before we will know if crime rate go down, because of more police presence.

9) <u>Moremoney in major citys.</u>

As method earlyer, money in most major citys is desportly needed. City are loosing money good residence to the suberbs. But the people who stay in the citys need more resources to stay abreast. Crime breed in the citys reason being, lack of money for program to help the poor. If crime is to subside in most american citys. More resources will be needed by states, and federal programs, to help the poor.

10) <u>Higher social programs in citys were there is high crime rates.</u>

Social program have always been fundmental to the citys. With the bush adminastration in The white house social programs are experted to be cut, with these cut, will bring more fundmental changes citys will have to find new ways to fund programs. if social programs are not yet started, such as walfare progams low econimcal housing, child care etc... crime in these area will (citys) sky rocket.

11) <u>Created more wealthy amercian</u>

Weath in amerca, is untainable if people don't have the expertise on how to obtain wealth. Crime breads mostly from povety. Povety will always be with us no matter how many programs are put in place.

Creating more wealth for young people between the ages of 18-24 will reduce crime rates in half.

12) Nation ID cards.

As used in engand, national ID cards will help keep track of crimminal movement from city to city national ID cards will also help police identify criminal more easier.

13) Better teknology for crime preventions.

We live in a busy world and there are billions of things happening as of this momment. Changes are taking place all over the country, One change which is Effecting all of us is Tecknology. Tecknology can play important role in crime prevention, such as using metal decters at bank and business this will greatly detane criminal activity in places were crime is fourmentable.

Conclusion- these are just a few examples on how to deture crime. As our society becomes more lawless we must find solution on how to fight crime. If our nation is to stay strong. We must find a way to put crime out of business.

Can the problem ever be solved-

In this section-we will look at the problem of crime and ask ourself can the problem ever be solved in the citys-

IN-the black community

Regions-East, West, North south

Conclusion-

City- Citys are the nest egg of crime. And we ask ourself, can the problem of crime in the city ever be solved. The answer is no citys will always have a high degree of crime reason being, popultion in citys then ever before. Crime rates in most metroptialty citys will only stay the same. And in most city crime will soar.

In the black community- Violent crime occurs in many places, and among all races, but I have just pointed out that it is heavily, concentrated in large cities. And therefore focus on the conditions of life for the youth of the innercity. To find the root cause of a high percentage of violent crime much has been written aobut innercity slums where crime and delinquency are bred. Socialscientists have analyzed slum conditions, and their causal ling to crime, and violence writers, and artists have dramatized the sordidness and frustrations of life in the inner cities, and a number of books prior to this one have produced comprehensive reports on this subject. In the black community crime are projected to stay pretty much the same as they were 10 years ago. Most law abinded blacks are tired of crime in there communitys. And want to find solutions to this problem as stated earlyer, most crimes are commited by black males between the ages of 16 to 24 reason being, most of these black youth, come from broken family, uslly one parent (Mother). With no father in the home, many of these young men turn to crime to fed themselves. Lack of selfesteem lack of knowledge of how to make a living. Gives them no other option but to trun to crime.

<u>Crime by regions-</u> Eastern region-

Crime in the Eastern region of the united state will stay the same population in the east has grow over the past five years. With this growth brings a diverse group of people. The easter region of the unnited state, has one third of the Amercan population. These people come from all different background, and income levels with these diffesity of people will bring a lot of crimnals activity. Something states, and police effectual are aware of.

<u>Western Region-</u> in the western region of the uninted states crime will grow; do to the population change in the new centrey. There are more people in the western part of the country then any other part of the uninted states. Most of these people are coming from other country such as Mexica, south amerca etc. most of these people are poor, and are in need of employment. There will be more then 50 million people in one state along(California) by the year 2008.

<u>Southern region-</u> in the southin part of the uninted state crime may increase do to climate, and high population growth, because of high enplyment rates. Crrimnal will have acsess to people with high standards of living. The southern region of the uninted states will be the nest egg of crime in the future.

Is the crime problem In Amerca getting better worse

The true level of crime in America is mystery, Reports to police compiled by the federal bureau of Investigation steadily increased for years after 1960 but leveled off in 2000, and actully declined in the six mouths of 2000 In 2001 tottal probably will exceed 1.9 million incidents when the final count is in

<Insert table, Crime and Population, page 162>

In this section we will look at crime in Amerca, and broke crime rate down to citys, suburea, south, west, north, East, In black communty white, community female, male and Conclusing

<u>The Citys =</u> The city have always been the nest egg of high crime rates. Most American city report Lower crime rate then 10 years ago.

<u>Areas were crime in citys are highest are.</u>

(1) lower econimic neiborhood = Income between 10,00 and 12,000 yearly.

(2) Neiborhood were there is a high degree of young people. between the age 15-24.

(3) Neiborhood were there is a large degree of unskilled workers.

(4) Neibohood were there is a large amont of alcohol, and drug use.

(5) Neiborhood were there is a lot of single parent mother.

(6) Neiborhood were there is a lot of single male, and female, ect.

<u>Motor vehicle theif In the Citys -</u> Motor vehecal theif in most major citys are up do to cairity reason. Motor Vehecle theif seem to be higher in lower econimic neibohoods. Where there is a high degree of young

people between the ages of 15 To 19. Days of the week Friday is highest.

Person to Person crime In the citys - Has always been high. Most person to person crimes occur among stanger. Most people who commited these crimes are young between the age of 18 To 24 The number one moutive in person to person crimes is money. Most of these crimes acure between 8 oclock in the even. And 2am at night. Days off the week Thursday and Friday, and saturday.

Homicide - In the cities - Homicide rate in most American citys are stabling off threwout the united state. Most homicide rate are climing were there is a high degree of unemployment, and Drug, and Alcohol use. all and all Homicide rate are about the same as they were 10 years ago In most Amercan Citys. And there will be no change In In the future.

Rape - In the citys Rape has stabled off over the past 10 years. Reason very Most Rape victem are white female between the age of 18 To 24. Most Rapest are young male between the age of 18 To 23. Most rape occur between 8 oclock at night to 12:am In the morning.

Burgalary in Amercan Citys = Burgalary in most Amercan citys has always been High. This is one area where crime rate in the city are climing Most burgarary occur between 8pm and 12:am. Most burgarer are between the age of 20 To 27. All and all crime rate are stabling off in some areas while in other area crime in the citys is going up.

Crime in the suburea - suburea crime intc. have always been low. But in reason years some suburea are climing in crime rate. we will take a breif look at each.

Person to Person Crime in suburb = Motorvehicle theift has stabled off over the vast 20 years In the suburbs, then this crime does a occurs. It usaly ocurs to white male over the age of 35. days of the Monday

Homcide in the Suburs - Homicde In the suburs occurs once in a while. Whenthen do occurs. They usually happen to white male under the age of 25. Days of the week Tuesday, and Friday. Mouth May and July.

Rape in the suburs - Rape is growing in some suburean areas. When rape does occur it usually happens to white female between the age of 18-24. Days of the week Friday, and Saturdays (mouth) July.

Burglary - Burglary is growing in the subura, reason very. Many beleive with High Income of most subburbing.-seem to bread crimnals in The suburea area. Most burglary In the suburs occurs between 9pm and 12am. Days of the week Friday, and Saturday.

Finnal suburean crime rate are stabling off all across the united states But with the suburbian population expected to double in the next 20years Crime rate are expected to double, this something law Inforcement agency are well aware of..

Rural Amerca - Rural Amecan crime rate have always been low Most crime rate that do occur are person to person crimes, which occurs 10 To Every 100,000 People. All other crime such as rape, burglary, homicde motor vehicle theft.. occurs 5 to 100,000 People.

Region of the united state.

   The south - Person to person, homiced, Rape, burglary motor vehicle Thef

   The West - Person to person, homiceds, Rape, burglary motorbehicle Thef

   The East - Person to person homiceds Rape, burglary motovehicle Theif

   The North - Person to person homiceds, Rape, burglary motorvehicle Thef

The south Person to person crimes = Person to Person crime occurs 1000 To Ever !00,000 In habits Most person to person crimes occurs to people between the age of 25 To 44 - Who lives in the southern region of the united states. Most of these person to person crimes occur To lower econimic people usally. 7: To 10: thousand dollar a year Income.

Most of these Person to person crimes occurs to males, and most crimes occurs between 9pm and 2am Most of these crime occur on Thursday, Friday, and saturday..And In the mouths of June and July.

Motorvehecal Theift - Motorvehecal Theift occurs To 20,000 To 100,000 Inhabites in souther region of the united state. When this crimes occurs Itcocuricty to white males Between the age of 25 To 35 Most days of the week when this crimes occurs is Thursday and Fridays and in the mouths of March, and April and July.

Burglary - Burglary is high In the southern region of the united state. Burglary occurs To 5,000 out of Ever 100,000 In habits Most burgalry victems are marred coupled, between the age of 27 To 44 With Incomes over 75,000 dollars commbined. Days of the week most burgarly occurs are. Thursday, and Friday. And In the mouths of Decmber, and Januarury. In the southern region of the united states.

Homicides In the south region - Homicides are up in the southern region of the united state. Many beleive Homicdes are up do to the high use of drugs in that region. Most Homicdes occur to black males between the age of 18 To 22. With Incomes of less then 10 Thousand a year. Days of the week when most homicdes occur are Friday, saturday between 8:oclack at Night and 2am morining. During The mouth of July, and August. And September.

Eastern Region of the Uninted states -

Person to person crimes - In the eastern region of the united states Is about the same as it was 10 years ago. When this crimes occurs it usally happens to males between the age of 25 to 35, with Income between 10 and 15,000 dollars a year. Days of the week Fridays and saturday between the time of 7pm and 12am. This crime usally occurs in the mouth of December, and Jannnary.

motor vehickle Theift In the eastern part of the country. Motor vehickle Theift is up in the eastern part of the united state. when this crime occurs, it uaally occurs To white males between the age of 30 To 40 years old. With Income over 40,000 dollars a years. This crime usually occurs on Tuesday, and Saturday between 8pm and 2am In the mouths May and June. In that region of the country.

Burgarly In the eastern region - burgalry is higher then it was in past years. In the Eastern region of the country when burgalry occurs it usally happen to marred couple between the age of 35 to 44 with Income between 45 thousand To 70 dollars a years.. The days most burgalry occurs In the Eastern region are, Thursday, and Friday between 8pm and 2am.

Rape In the eastern region - Rape In the eastern Region of country Is stabling off. When rape occurs, it usually occurs to white female with income between 30 to 40 thousand a year. The averge age of most victem are 20 To 27 years of age. Most raps occurs between the hours of 9pm and 2am in that region of the country

Homicde in the Eastern region - Homicde Have stabled off over the past few years In the Eastern region of the country. When homicde occurs They occur to Male between the age of 20 to 35 with Income level between 10 thousand dollor To 15 thousand. Most Homicdes occur between 9pm To 2pm on Fridays and saturday in the mouths off December to January.

The Northern Region of united states - Person to Person Crime

Person to Person crimes have stabled off in The Norther region of the country. When this crime does occur up north occurs mostly To white male between the age of 22 To 28. With Income of 15 thousand To 20,000 per year. Most of these crimes occur between 7pm To 3am In the morning. On Thursday and Friday evening between the mouths of July and August.

Motor Vehicle Theift In the Northern region - <Motor vehicle Theif has stabled off In the northern region of the country when this crime does occur-it effect all people of all age groups equally. Most Motor vehicle theif occur on tuesday, and thursday and between 8pm and 1am in the morning. ANd between the mouths of January and March.

<u>Burgarey In the North</u> - Burgalary In The Northern part of the country has stabled off in reason years. Buglery effects people of all Incomes. Most burgaoly in North occurs at 9pm To 3am In the morning. Most days burgarly occurs are on, Thursday and Friday evening in the North. Between the mouths of July and December.

<u>Rape In the Norther part of the country -</u> Rape in the Norther part of the country is about the same as it was 10 years ago. Most rape victems are white female between the age of 18 to 22. With Income of less than 1 7 thousand a year. Most rape occur between 9pm To 1am In the morning. Between Mondays, and Thursday. Between the mouths of July and August

<u>Homicdes In the Norther part of the country</u> Homcide are lower In the Norther part of the country then In past years. Homicede effects all Genders In all age groups. Most homiceds occur In the even hours. In the northern part of the country. Between 10 oclock To 3am in the morning Mostly in the mouths of December, and Febuarary. On Friday evening.

<u>Western region of the united state person to person crime</u>

Person To Person crimes occur In the western part of the united state on a daily basses. Most of these crimes effeted male between the age of 18 To 24. Most of these person to person Crimes occur between the hours of 9pm To 2am In the morning. The days of the week when these crimes occur most are. Thursday and saturday between the mouths of July, and December In that region of the country.

<u>Motor Vehicle Theft In the wester igion of the united states</u>

Motor Vehicle Theft is higher in the western part of the united states Then in any other part of the country. Motor Vehicle theft occurs To 10,000 out of ever 100,000 Inhabits. Motor Vehicle theft occurs mostly In the western region of the country. between 9pm to 2am on Friday, and saturday evens. Between the mouths of July, and August. When most Vehicle theft occurs there.

Burgalary In the western region of the united states

Burgalary Is up in the western region of the country reason very Most burgalary occur to 15,000 out of Ever 100,000 Inhabits. Most burgary occurs In the western region of the united state between 9pm To 2am In the morning. Days of the most burgarary In that region of the country are Thursdays, and Friday In the mouths of June, and July. When most burgalary occur.

Rape In the western region of the country -

Raper has stabbled off In the western region of the united states. Rape occurs to 500 out of ever 100,000 Inhabits. Most rape victems are white females between the age of 19 To 23. Most rape occur there between the hours of 10 oclock in the evening, and 12:30 In the morning. The Days of the week when most rape occurs are Tuesday, and Friday, and saturday. Between the mouths of July and December.

Homicedes in western region f the united states.

Homicedes in the western region of the united state are higher than they were 10 or 20 years ago. Most Homicedes occur between 9pm and 1am In the morning. The Days most homicedes occur in the West are. Fridays and Saturday. between the mouths of July, and August. Finnal crimes rate vary from region to region Depending on the curumctance. The Day the week. The time and location. Note data collected from police department across the country.

Crime rates in the black community - by regions

Homicedes- 10- out of 100,000 people

Rape- 5 out of 100,000 people

Burgary- 25 out of 100,000 people

Person To Person- 7 out of 100,000 people

Motor Vehecal Theift- 8 out of 100,000 people

South- 7 out of 100,000 people

North- 5 out of 100,000 people

East- 15 out of 100,000 people

West- 10 out of 100,000 people

Homicedes In the black community In the south

Homicedes In the black community In the southern part of The united state is higher then 10 years ago. Most homicedes are commited by black males between the age of 18 To 21 Most homicedes Victems are also black male in the same age group. Most black male who commited homiceds are In the lower ecnicmic bracket. Most Homicede commited by black male In the south occur between 9pm and 1am. On saturday and Friday. In the mouths of December, and July.

Rape In the black commuty In the souther region of the country

Rape in the black communty In the south has stabled off over the past 20 years. When rape occurs, It occurs to black female between the age of 14 To 19. Most black females who are raped are In the lower, econmic bracket. With Income less then 10 thousand a year. Days of the week most rapes occur In the south are Saturday, and Friday. between 9pm and 1am. In the mouths of August, and December.

Burgalary In the black communty In the south -

Burgalary is up in the souther region of the united state. Most bugarery are young black males between the age of 15 To 21. With Income of less then 10 thousand a year. Most burgarly occur between 1pm and 12:am In the morning. Most days burgarly occur are Thursday and Fridays. Between the mouths of July and December. In the black community In the south.

Person to Person crime In the south In the black communty

Person to person crime occurs In the south In the black communty on a dailey bases, 10,000 out of ever 100,000 In habits are victem of Person to Person crimes. Most of these crime occur to black males between the age of 19 To 23 With Income of less than 10 Thousand a year. The time when most of these person to person crimes occur are

8pm In the evening to 1: oclock In the morning. And between the mouths of December and May.

<u>Motor Vehicle Theft In black communty In the south.</u>

Motor Vehicle Theft In the black communty is highes there then other region of the country. Motor Vehivle Theift occurs to 10,000 To ever 100,000 Inhabites. Most Motor Vehicle theif occurs to black males between the age of 22 To 30 years of age. With Income levels. between 15 thousand To 20 Tousand a year. Time of the day when most motor vehicle are stolen In the south are, 7:30 in the evening to 11:30 In the evening. On Tuesdays and Saturdays In the mouths of July and August.

<u>Crime rates In the Norther part of the united state In the black commiteds</u>

<u>Homicedes</u> -

Homicedes In the black community are stabling off In the Norther part of the country-most Homicedes victem are black male between the age of 17 To 24. With Income of less then 10 thousand dollor a year. out of ever 100,000 Inhabits 2,000 are Homicedes victems. Most Homicede occur In large city. Between 9pm To 3am on Friday, and saturday, between the mouths of December and Janarury.

<u>burgarlary</u> -

burgarlary occurs to many blacks on a dailey bases In the Norther region of the country. Most burgarly occur In low Income neiborhood. Where Income are less then 10 Thousand a year. days of the week when most burgarly occur are Saturday, and Tuesday. at 8oclock in The evening to 2am In the morning During the mouths of November to December.

<u>rape</u>

Rape Is about the same as it was 10 years ago In the North Rape victem in the black commited are young women between 19 To 27. 500 out of every 100,000 Inhabitted are rape victem there most of these victem are In the low econimic bracket beteen with 7 to 10 Thousand dollor a year. Most rape occure there between 9pm to 2am In the morning on Thursday and Friday between June and July.

Person to Person crime - In the North

Person to person crime, are about the same as they were 10 years ago In black Northern communty. 10,000 Thousand out of every 100,000 habites are a victem of Person to person crime. Most person to person crime victem are young black male between the age of 18 To 21 years old. With annually Income of less then 10 thousand dollors a year. Most person to person crimeIn norther black community. Are between 8pm To 2am In the morning and on Wensday, and Saturday between the mouths of december, and Jauarary

Motor Vehicle Theift In black communty In the south region

Motor vehicle theif In black communty In the North is about the same as In the past 5 thousand out of every 100,000 Inhabites are victem of motor vehicle Theif in the black community. In the North. Time of day of most theifs are 9am to 1pm in the morning. During the days of Tuesday and wendedays In the mouths of May and September.

Crime In the black community In the East

burgarlary -

Burgarlary has been stabley In most black communty out East over the past few decades. Burgalary effected 7 Thousand out of ever 100,000 Inhabites. In black community there. Most burgarery occur between 8pm to 11:30 on Thursday and Tuesday. between the mouths of August and September and December.

Homicdes -

Homicdes In black community out East has stabled off In reason years. Most Homicede victem are young black male between the age of 18 To 22, with Income of less then 15 thousand a year. Most homiceds occur in major city out east between 9pm and 11:30 pm on Thursday and Friday on the mouths of July and December.

Person to Person crime in the east in the black communty

Person to person crime out east has stabled off in eason years. Person to person crime occurs to 5,000 out of every 100,000 Inhabites In that region. Most victem of person to person crime in the black community out east are young male between the age of 19 To 23. with income of less then 15,000 per year. Most person to person crime occur between 7pm and 12pm In the morning. between the mouths of July and August. out east.

Motor vehical theif In black community out east =

Motor vehical theif is up in eastern black community. Motor vehical Theif occurs to 8,000, out of every 100,000 inhabites. Motor vehical theif occurs toon Tuesday and Thursday between 8pm and 1am between the mouths of August and September. When this crime occurs most. in that region.

rape In the black community out east - Rape out east is the same as usally- 3,000 out of every 100,000 black female between the age of 18 To 21 are rape victem. Majorty of Rape victem are low income black female with Income of less then 10,000 a year. Most rape occur between 8pm and 1:am on Thursday and Saturday between the mouths of July and August.

Can the problem ever be solved

Northern region-The northern region of the united state. crime will stay the same. Reason being, Population will stay the same, and Income levels will not change.

<u>Conclusion</u> Crime in America is forcing federal, state and local government officials to spend billions of dollors on police pretection, prison, and companies to purchase massive amounts of private protection. At the same time homicide, rape, burglary. and assaults increase health care spending, and lead to lost wages. and productivity consulted economist, and criminal Justice experts around the Country in order to estimate the annual cost of crime in the united states the staggering price tag 174 billion a year.

The future of crime

In this section we will look at crime in 3 areas

(1)Citys.

(2)tecknology.

(3)Crime 100 years from know.

4 Conclusion.

And were crime will be in the future in these areas.

(1) citys - Projections prepared by the national commission on population growth, and the american Future indicate that the united states will continue to become more urbanized over the next several decades. In 1990 about 71 percent of all Americans lived in metropolitan areas by the year 2008 the population Cominission expects 85 percent of the population to be living in metroplitan areas. The increase in most metropolition areas will be in suburbs. Rather than in central cities. While estimates of the magnitude of population changes may vary as projection, are up dated the direction is clear. The population density of central cities will not change drastically, and parts of surrounding suburbs will become more dense. This is significant in light of the historical association between population density, and crime rates. Robbery, burglary, and other property crime rates are considerably higher in central cities than in suburbs, or rural areas. However violent crim, and burglary rates have been rising faster in the suburbs already are beginning to feel crimiogenic effects of steadily increasing urbanization.

Population Mobility -

The move to urban areas will bring with it not only pressure and opportunities for anti social behavior, but also the loss of a sense of community that comes with wide spread mobility. The extend, and impact of transiency in the population has been explored recently by Vance Packard, who estimates that at least a fifth of all Americans move one, or more times each year, and the pace of the movement of Americans is still increasing Pervasive movement produces rootlessness which in turn leads to a sense of anonymity that is felt by segments of large urban populations. A lack of common experience in a crowded, but transient populacee makes the organization of citizen crime prevention efforts more difficult. It also hinders the development of close police community relations. Rootlessness, or mobility may also be a factor leading to criminality a longitudinal study of delinguent males in Philadephia, PA found that one of the cariables significantly associated with Police contacts especially repeated contacts, was degree of school, and residential mobility- the more mobility, the more police contacts. Although there may be several explanation for this association, one of the most likely is that high mobility lessens ordinary community ties that restrain delinguency-prone you this from illegal acts In short, Increaseing population mobility is likely to contribution to Americas crime problems during the next decade Finnal, Certain Citys such as east saint Louest will be abanded. Because crime is so bad there. So The future of crime in that city has no future.

Tecknology Future of crime - In this section we will look at tecknology involvement with crime In the future. We will look at three areas there are.

Video camera-

microscope -

D.N.A-

Conclusion -

Video camera -> The video movement started in California. The movement began with the Rodney King, and Reginal Denny tapes Like images of the challenger disater, or the Zapruder film, these video clips instantly burned into our nations conscioosness. First four Los Angeles police officers pound Rodney King. Then, Damian Williams.

savagely attackss Reginold Denny, after denny is pulled out of is truck. The tapes evoked the worst image from Americas appalling record on raciism lynching police. brutalilty. Both tape demanded resounding finding of guilty But there was also a sense of relief. Thanks god for the video. The video camera is one of the most powerful intrument in tecknology today. Video camera can be used to recall Information, which is placed on film. This is one tecknology which will be used for many years. To come. To help to deter crime in owe soceity

Microscope - The microscope was one of the earliest tools used for the development of scientific evidence. By microanalysis. The scientist is able to examine physical evidence under such magnifications that would not be possible with only the naked eye. The comparison microscope is an invaluable improement over the ordinary microscope. The comparison microscope permits the examination and coparsison of two objects at the same time. In the 1960s another new and highly sophisticated tool became available to crime laboratories. The scanning electronic microscope, or sem is an expensive piece of electronic equiptment. The sem permits observations of the surface of materials at magnifications up to 140,000 times the orginal size. It also permits an elemental analysis of any portion of material in concentrations as low as one part per million. This would means for example, that arsenic, or lead could be detected in a single red blood cell. It is estimated that it would take 4000 red blood cells laid end to end to equal one inch. The microscope has been used to solve many crime. From around The world. And is one tool which will be used for many years to come. To help solve crimes. In own socity

D.N.A testing - Everyone has DNA In There blood. DNA makes that person diffrent then any other person. DNA has been used To solve many crimes, such as the O.J. Simpon trials and other high profile cases. D.N.A is one of the highest used tecknology today. And this is one tecknology criminal are very aware of. DNA is stored on databasees Finnal, There are other areas were tecknology plays a inmortant part in crime such as Fingerprinting, wiretapping, electronicall, surveilance and Furmzik Evedence and Mardia Law, Based upon which city and state you live in check In your local Libary for books on the subject. On DNA

Crime a hundred years from now - One hundred years from now crime looks bleak. If you think crime is bad now. wait to you here projection of the future. here are a list of area were crime will take its tool.

Citys-

  TV Radio Newspapers-

  siberspace -

  Cumputer system-

  Money-

  Natial Crefew-

  man against woman-

  live expectence->

  social program->

  Commitys->

  blacks against white->

  food and water supplys->

  on Goverment->

Conclusion->

Citys -> Citys will become more dangers. They (citys) will be the battle ground for police, and national guards against millions of criminals, as resourse become less Millions of people will turn to crime to support them selves. Gangs and drugs will be the norm, for criminal a hundred year from now. The police will be cut manned. Because of all the criminal activity going onion a daily basis

Tv Radio News papers= 100 hundred years from now Tv Radio newspapers, will be state ran. All information we reseved will be cenersed. Reason being, Criminal have eyes, ears to see and to lisen, And state run program will be monterd to demand criminal activity.

Siber space - During the reagan administration. Ronald reagan dreamed of of plan- to stop sovet missile from hitting the united states. This plan was called star wars. This plan will also be used to keep track of criminals movement. by the year 3000 Siber space will be in effecte by computer use.

Computer system - A hundred years from now. Computer systems will be more advanced. Computer system will be able to store Invormation on (data bases), on criminal for decades. Computer system will be able to keep track of criminal who are on probation, and Parole, and which Criminal are the most dangers, and which are not. Computer system, are the number one tool which will be used to keep track of criminal in the future.

Money - Money will be the number one element of need in the next 100 years. For people who dont have money in the future Crime. will be there only alternative. Money will be so pwerful 100 years from now. We will be living in a society of the haves, and the have nots. And the have nots will be The criminal from all cornes of the Globe and crime rate will soar mostly for poor people In owr majory citys. Threw out The united state and The world

National Curfews -> 100 years from now. We will be living in a time were people will have to be inside by eleven oclock, no person will be aloud on the street after that time. If a person is on the street after that time. They will be taking as a criminal, unless They have work permits.

Man against Women - 100 years from now man, and women will be so far apart there will be no room for love. Women will fear men, because of high crimnal activity through out many community million of men will become lovers to only one thing. and that thing is crime.

Live expectence - live expetence will be cut short do to high crime rates in certain citys. With the explosion of hand guns and more crimnal on the street then ever before. Live expectence will be cut. Mostly amoug black males between the age of 18 to 25. In the community were they live

<u>Social programs</u> - Will be a thing of the past. There will be no free money in the next 100 years. With these cuts will being more crime. If state goverment want crime to ccutail In the next hundred years. They must restore social program for the poor.

<u>Communitys</u> - Every community in the world will have neiborhood watch program. Do to high crime rates in certain communitys. Community watch programs, are very Inpatant to the people who live in them. Without these program. People will become victems to crimes 10 times more then with out them.

<u>Blacks against white</u> - 100 years from now there will be racial wars, black and white will be puninting there fingers at each other. Crimnal will take advantage of this by praying on the waek in both racees. And people of color In other races.

<u>food and water</u> - Both food, and water will be rehashed. scarisity will occur in these basic nessity. Crimnal will take advantage of these scarisity by robbing robing grocery stores. banks, Breaking in people home, stealing what ever they can get there hands on. Crimnals will use there criminal instinct to survive in a world gone mad.

<u>Goverment Control of people.</u> People are free to go where they want to go and when, But this wont be the case one hundred years from now. Goverment will control people movement when they can go, and where. Crime would have gotten so bad In the future People will have distict mark on there fore heads. (Mark of the Beast) distributed by goverment. People will have these marks to indicate who they are there, age, there live style, ect. there marks will distinguish criminal from none crimnals. If you don't have the mark, goverment, and state officials will take you as a criminal, and place you in house arrest. This will be goverment way of dealing with crime.

<u>Conclusion</u> -> This is a gloomie forecast of the future no man can realy project the future. It will be up to man to change its own future. Man is the ruler of all thing. Only he can change owr path, and make it better, or worse for all of us, and for owr generations. Let there be no room for don't, crime will not be tolerated in the future, We can't waste not

one person to criminal activity. With 95 million more people comming into the world each year. Resourse will become, scares with less resouse, means more crime. more crime more vilence. There is a dangers world we live in No matter where you go in the world. You may find yourself a victem of crime. There are million of criminal activty which take place every day. From purse snaching. burglaries, hommiced, muging bank robbery, raping ect. Criminal are busyer then ever, final as only way out for million of people. If Goverment, and state leaders don't find a answer to Amercan crime problem. We will be living in a place were we will loose owr freedom because crime will be the norm in owr society.

Conclusion

Violent crime is heading straight toward us. Crime is no more common in some places its less so than others. But is has been to common all along. And the impact cumulations Every new victem is added to the millions before. The headlines of 2005 have shown that crime can strick any wherre. Every night local newscast in the nations large metropolition areeas, show that violent crime is especially consentrated in black underclass communities. In 39 percent of murders were committed in 25 cential cities with just 12 Percent of the population. Detroit, and washington had murder rates 12 to 16 times higher than those of their suburbs. Politicians solutions can help reduce crime in the larger comunurty. But something more is needed to reduce the sickening violence in poor communnities where violence, and sexual predation can be overwhelming Gun-control laws will surely prevent some crimes, But we dont want to become a gunless nation. Longer prison sentences, and fewer paroles, plus laws requiring the lifetime imprisonment of violent felons convicted three times will help prevent other crimes. But what of the neighborhoods where the criminals are in charge? The key here may be to desanction crime, to tell the young males everyone knows are criminals that they can be stoped. So many violent criminals are repeat offenders estimates range from 50 percent up - it is inevitable that many former prisoners as well as defendants awaiting trail, and convicts on probation will be arrested for new crimes Critics change that the system remains unaccountable justice professionals respound that their record of singling out of persons arrested for violent crimes about 17 percent have charges pending for other crimes 13 percent more are on probation on parole, or other wise already ties up in the justice system. The federal government recently launched massive research that will try to determine how violent behavior can be short circuited. The results will come none too soon by the year

2005. The number of 15 to 19 year old the violence-prone age group will increase by 23 percent unless a way is found to break the vicious cycle of violence. Many fear that will mean the emergence of an even larger group of stone killer. Many experts say there are larger trends that abet the rise of coldblooded killers There are the penal policies that allow many of the most violent criminals to return to their homes well before sentence are up. One thing is certain America is conserrded soft on crime. As we inter the new year crime is at the forefront on ever ones mind. The bush administration, has placed crime high on it prority list. All and all. This is still a law abinded country. most people dint go around raping, and robing, ect. Most of us still get along with each other. But there are million of people who wake up with crime on there minds. We all have choosees to make in owr own lives, such as who we want to marrie, where we want to live where we want to work ect. But please dont choose a live of crime. We all only have, one live to live. Once it over you can never come back. Make the right choosees in live, But whatever chose you make. Please don't choose a live of crime. Crime has gotten billion of people living in fear, Scared to walk the street, scared to visted family and Friends ect. People from all walks of live want to live a safe live. We can't let crimnal take over owr society. We must find a soulution to this age old problem. If not, we will be living in a third world country. If owr society survey, we must all be retrained to be better people. We live in a vilent society, were people from all age groups, and colors are out of control. There is alot of dislike in the world blacks against, white, Rich against poor, But for us to coexist, we must learn to live with each other. If we don't owr world will be place of turmoil. Man has a lot of time on his hand, planty of time to get owr world in order There will always be a tomorrow. So with this knowledge we can spent owr time making this world a better place for all of us. Theres good, and evil in all of us, being that we are diffrent, but yet the same. We all have owr on feiw of live, and how we want to live it. If you want to have a good live. Stay away from people Who advacted crimnal activity. Crimnal are united guess who come over for dinner. And with millions of crimnals out there, you may not be able to fed them all. Crimnal are low Quality people. With low values, low moral, and are living a live with no goels. Drifting from day to day

146

with no guidence, and no hope. Crimnal are lonley people looking for anyone to hage with. To help them with there crimnal activity. Crimnal have lost touch with reality. They dont know day from night. They are sick and in need of treatment. Crimnal make bad decision at the wrong time. Crimnal have to exept the fact that this is real live. This is not a game. But yet crimnal take live as a game, Running from city to city spreading lyes and desiption. Crimnals are running out of time, reason being The cards are stagged against them, meaning No one want crimnals arounf them. They look for friends, But ever were they go they reseve rejection. Crimmnals are out dated, why? because crime is out dated. No one wants to grow-up to be a crimnal. The million of crimnal who are still out there, want to change there lives. Crimmnal Have there backs against the wall why? because crime is becomeing obsolete No one wants crimnal on the job. In there community In there lives, People don't want crimmnal on The planeted.

After all, crimnal are the ones starting all the trouble in todays world. Most of us are law abinded citizens. We follow the Rules, and regulation set up by man. But crimnal dont want to follow rules. They want to make there own rules. They feel the world evolves around them. But this is not true, we all have to follow rule set by man. If we don't, we will be living in a lawless society. Society is not perfect, but it is all we have, and crimnal must learn to follow soceity rules. Soceity must find a new business for crimnal to go into. Criminal are people who are out of control. Crimnal Think they can do what they want to do. Whenever they want to. But live does not work that way. Crimnal think they are bad. But they are not bad. There people just like me, and you. People from all walks of live professinal and non professinal want to see the end of crime. Crime has been a problem in owr society sence plymouth rock.Crimnnals need these elements to change there live of crime.

(1) A job - or business.

(2) sel esteen.

(3) A place to live were they can call home.

(4) Highermoral - about them selfs, and others.

(5) Things to do with there time.

(6) A loving spouce, or child.

(7) A good education.

(1) <u>A Job, or business</u> - Everyone need some way to support themself ether a job, or business, or both. Crimnal also need a way to support themselfs. Placing crimnals in job program will help them to cope better with real live. Having a job will give them more meaning to there live. A job with a live able wadge. Will make them feel better about themself.

<u>Sel esteem</u> - Crimnal don't feel highly about themselfs. So they turn to crime to get attenuation. crimnal needs selestee to modivatated themself, that theyare somebody instead of a nobody.

<u>A Place to live were they can call Home</u> - Everone needs a place to live Even crimnals. Crimnals send most of there time on the streets, or in jail. A place to live were they can call home. Will greatly imrove there standard of living. Goverment housing can help crimnal get off the streeets and into a place where they can call home.

<u>Higher moral about themselfs and others</u> - Crimnal need things to do with there time. being on the street 90 percent The time, brings trouble. With to much free time on there hands. Once again idleness brings crime.

<u>Loving spouce, or child</u> -> Every body needs some body to care for them, even crimnals. By having a spuce or child will enable the crimnal to have more meaning in live. remember, love will keep us together.

<u>A Good education</u> -> Everybody needs a good education To compete in todays world. Most crimnals are high school dropout, or have no education at all. Without a good education, crimnals cannot compete in todays world. Having a good education will enable the crimnal to compete in a highly complex system. Remember most crimnal are males, Not to say there are not female crimnal, but are over represend by males. As you can see, crimnals lack the basic nessaty in live which we all need to sirvive As stated early, vilet crime is the numeber 1 problem facing society today. Every 10 seconds someone dies In the

country, and 40% of time its because of vilet crime. Every 6 seconds a women is rapped, Every 50 seconds some one is Assailed. Every day a child is criminally abducted. And the list goes one and on. One time is all it takes imagine how you would feel if someone in your family became one of these statistics. Why Risk what could happen when it so easy to prevent. Your live is very important. So Don't let A crimnal take your live. I would like to see the day were there is no lost of humman live to crime. A day when we all can coexist without the fear a crime and vilence.

No person can save the world, but you can make it a better place by saying no to crime no to drugs. If you set example to other bye saying no, other people will also say no. The harts, and minds of men ever where what to see a tend to crime. As we bottle Issues today such as crime, and vilence, We must not forget. These Issue have always been with us Million of people are getting tired of the struggles of live Meaning Job, children, spouce, ect. And dealing with the crime Issue only make things worse. With all the problem facing todays world. why do we as a society have to continue to seal with crime Issue. As we male into the new mullion, men and women must stand tall to fight back against crime. We will survive this crime blitz. After all we must because, we are all In the same boat. If we could live a happy life by being thankful that we are here. Say yes to live, and no to crime. Ent, drink, and be marry. Is whats live is all about. Keep the faith. And you will live great live. Instead of living a live of crime. Lets put crime behind us, and go forward to more serious matters. Dont be a loser in life, be a winner. By being a prouductive member of socety. Have a high Quality live. Who want to live 50, 60, 75 years as a crimmnal, when you can be a successful person. Yes death, and taxes is inevitable, but wile we are here, lets enjoy it. Set your goal wisely To be the best you can be. This strong thing we all infered call live, can be fun, exciting finnal, the events of sept 11 has changed the minds of billions of men and women around the world. This one event have shown the world that crime has gotten out of control Osamabin Laden and his gang of terrosit is believed to be the prime suspect In this crime against Amerca. With this event. The govermment has Declared war on terrorists. This will give the goverment more power to search and seize than ever before. That means innocent people are at risk of being trapped in the federal goverment wide net Be careful THe goverment may finger you. Finnal we live in a age of cirle killer Rasism, sexual abuse, Robbery, mugging, drug dealing, child abuse, Prostitution, credit card fraud, paticulaorpotan, white collor crime, and the list goes on and on. With all this crime going on around us. We must evaluated owr lives and we must say to owrself. want do we realy want out of live. A Good Job, a house, a loving spouce, travel ect But for the majority of us we all want to be productive member of society by saying no to crime. Longevity is the key in live By. Staying strong and keep the faith. As the saying goes see no evil speak no evil, hear no evil, Ever real blooded Amercan want to see the end of crime in owr lives All 6 billions of us are in world together to win the war on crime God save owr planted.

Protecting yourself and your family members from burglary assult and crime ect write for the crime Resistance book Public affairs Dept Room 6236 FBI 10th and 2 Pennsylvania Ave washington DC 20535 Also you can right A book of crime prevention Methods and ideas The National Crime Prevention Council 1700 k st NW 2nd Floor washington DC 20006817 you will be glad you did.

Alternative Reading Sources

Crime and the Legal Process - chamblis William Mcgraw Hill

Correction in America - Allen
Publishing   Simosen Mac Milliam

Criminal Evidence - Gurder Thomas   West Publishing Co

Criminal Law Pricipal and cases
Publishing Co   Gurder Thomas West

Criminal Law and Procedure   Bons Robert Mcgraw Hill

Criminolgy
Publishing   Vorenberg James West

American Constitution Laws   Martin Shpiro Roce J Tresolini